D0044131

Basic Buddhist Concepts

Basic Buddhist Concepts

KOGEN MIZUNO

translated by
Charles S. Terry
and
Richard L. Gage

KOSEI PUBLISHING CO. • Tokyo

Reproduced on the front cover is a medallion from the stone
railing surrounding an ancient stupa at Bharhut, north-central
India. The carving dates back to the first century B.C. The
bo tree in the center of the medallion symbolizes
the Buddha. Photo by Isamu Maruyama.

This book was originally published in Japanese
under the title *Bukkyō to wa Nanika*.

Editing, book design, typography, and cover design by
EDS Inc., Editorial & Design Services.
The text of this book is set in a computer version of Melior
with a computer version of Optima for display.

First English edition, 1987
Third printing, 1992

Published by Kōsei Publishing Co.,
Kōsei Building, 2-7-1 Wada, Suginami-ku, Tokyo 166 Japan.
Copyright © 1965 by Kōgen Mizuno, 1987 by Kōsei Publishing Co.;
all rights reserved. Printed in Japan.

ISBN 4-333-01203-1   LCC 87-670046

Contents

PREFACE   7

1   THE HISTORICAL CONTEXT   13
Primitive Buddhism, *13*   Sectarian Buddhism, *18*
Early Mahayana Buddhism, *26*
Middle-Period Mahayana Buddhism, *31*
Late Mahayana Buddhism, *35*

2   THE FUNDAMENTALS OF
SHAKYAMUNI'S PHILOSOPHY   39
The Three Treasures, *39*   Buddhism as Philosophy, *41*
The Seals of the Law, *44*
Views of Humankind and Fate, *50*   Causation, *54*

3   THE TWELVE-LINKED CHAIN OF
DEPENDENT ORIGINATION   59
An Overview, *60*   The First Three Links, *64*
The Remaining Nine Links, *66*
Dual Dependent Origination, *69*
Dependent Origination and Fate, *70*
Dependent Origination and Karmic Rewards, *72*
Inexhaustible Interrelations, *76*

4 THE PATHWAY TO FAITH 81
The Gateway to Faith, 83
Mistaken Theories of Causation, 87

5 THE RELIGIOUS SPIRIT 91
Awakening, 91 Development, 93
The Four Indestructible Objects of Faith, 97
The Triple Doctrine and the Four
Indestructible Objects of Faith, 101

6 THE FOUR NOBLE TRUTHS 105
The Meaning of the Four Noble Truths, 105
Setting the Wheel of the Law in Motion, 108
Suffering, 111 Judging Impermanence Correctly, 113
The Cause of Suffering, 115
Freedom from Suffering, 119
The Way to Eliminate Suffering, 121

7 THE EIGHTFOLD PATH 129
Right Views, Right Thought, 130
Right Speech, Right Action, Right Livelihood, 131
Right Effort, Right Mindfulness, Right Meditation, 133
Other Views of the Path, 135

8 THE THREEFOLD LEARNING 139
Precepts, 139 Precepts in Mahayana Buddhism, 141
Fundamentals of Meditation, 144
Other *Dhyana*, 148 Meditation Before Buddhism, 150
Shakyamuni and Meditation, 153
Buddhist Meditation, 156 Wisdom, 159
Buddhist Ideals, 162

GLOSSARY-INDEX 167

Preface

In its more than twenty-five hundred years of history, Buddhism has acquired an extraordinarily complicated body of doctrines that vary from sect to sect throughout Hinayana and Mahayana, the religion's two main streams. Grasping all of its content is extremely difficult. In this book, to make entry into the field easier for the inexperienced, I have attempted to cut through sectarian differences and to set forth basic truths common to all Buddhism. My approach is justified since, in its purest form, Buddhism inclines to no particular group or sect but reveals the universal human condition. In this sense, it is the ideal religion for the future. A person who understands its truth, even though he or she lacks knowledge of special doctrinal terms and vocabulary, cannot fail to see that Buddhism is correct and applicable to all places and times.

Buddhism is more a matter of finding a truth that guides faith and practice and serves as a guideline in daily life than a purely intellectual field of study. Nonetheless, the pursuit of that truth necessarily entails knowledge of certain fundamental theories and doctrines. This book deals with such matters from the standpoint of Buddhism as a whole, with special reference to primitive Buddhist teachings, which are representative of the fundamental world view of the entire religion.

Immature myself in both faith and religious practice, I am perhaps presumptuous in writing a book designed to guide others in these matters. But religion—and especially Buddhism, which has no peer for excellence in rationality, ethical and moral teachings, and religious faith—is of such importance to humanity at the present time that, my own shortcomings aside, I will be very happy if this work can introduce others to Buddhist truth.

The Japanese-language original of this book was a compilation of a series of articles first published in the journal *Daihōrin* (Great Wheel of the Law), starting in 1960. Though extensively revised before publication in book form, the text nonetheless retains some of the repetitions, overlappings, and abrupt changes of topic that are not out of place in a magazine serial. Some of the repetition was deliberate, for the sake of emphasis; the rest reflects the original process of composition, and for this I ask the reader's indulgence.

Individual interpretations of Buddhism alter and grow with time. This book contains ideas different from those I have presented elsewhere and even some opinions with which I no longer completely agree. In other words, it reveals developments in my own viewpoint over the passing years.

Because I intended this book for the reader who may have no special knowledge but is nonetheless interested in learning something about Buddhist philosophy, I have tried to make sometimes challenging material as accessible as possible. To this end, I have used simplified transliterations of Pali and Sanskrit words throughout. Thus the reader will find, for example, Shakyamuni, Rajagriha, and *trishna* instead of the scholarly Śākyamuni, Rājagṛha, and *tṛṣṇā*, which can appear both daunting and unpronounceable.

However, I have included the orthodox transliterations of all such words in the glossary-index.

For readers of a scholarly bent, I should mention that I have freely used both Pali and Sanskrit words in the text, depending on what is appropriate in the context. In discussing concepts and documents of the Southern (or Hinayana) Buddhist tradition, I use Pali, the language in which its texts were recorded. For Northern (or Mahayana) concepts and documents, I use Sanskrit. But such usage is not always consistent, for I have occasionally used the more familiar or usual form of a word without regard for its linguistic context.

I have followed the current scholarly practice of using the Wade-Giles system to romanize Chinese words in works dealing with the period before the 1949 revolution and the new pinyin system of romanization in works concerning the period after 1949.

Finally, I have used the terms Mahayana and Hinayana to refer to Northern and Southern Buddhism, respectively. Though Hinayana (literally, "Small Vehicle") was a derogatory term coined by Mahayana ("Great Vehicle") Buddhists, I use it because it refers to all the sects of the Southern Buddhist tradition. (Theravada, the term often used in contrast to Mahayana, is the name of only a single Southern Buddhist sect.)

Basic Buddhist Concepts

1 The Historical Context

Buddhism was founded about twenty-five hundred years ago in northeastern India by Shakyamuni, the Sage of the Shakya Tribe, who attained perfect enlightenment and became the Buddha, the Enlightened One. The history of Indian Buddhism may be divided into five periods: (1) the age of primitive Buddhism, which lasted from the time of Shakyamuni (c. 560–c. 480 B.C.) until the division of Buddhism into sects (about 300 B.C.); (2) the age of sectarian Buddhism, which lasted from about 300 B.C. until the beginning of the first century A.D.; (3) the early period of Mahayana Buddhism, which lasted from the beginning of the first century A.D. until about 300; (4) the middle period of Mahayana Buddhism, which lasted from about 300 to about 700; and (5) the late period of Mahayana Buddhism, which lasted from about 700 to the early thirteenth century.

The age of primitive Buddhism lasted from the time of the Buddha's enlightenment until the schism that separated the faith into sects. The precise limits of the period are difficult to establish. Although the schism at its close can be said with fair certainty to have occurred in the time of the Mauryan emperor Ashoka, who reigned from about

13

273 to about 232 B.C., dates associated with the life of the
Buddha are less definite. The traditions of both Northern
(Mahayana) and Southern (Hinayana) Buddhism hold that
the Buddha lived to be eighty and that he had achieved
enlightenment at the age of thirty-five. But while the Southern tradition claims that he died 218 years before the ac-
cession of Ashoka, the Northern tradition insists that only
approximately a hundred years elapsed between the two
events. In other words, the primitive period lasted either
about a century and a half or about two and a half centuries, depending on which of the two versions is accepted.
As it happens, a difference of a hundred years or so has no
great bearing on the characteristics of the early religion.
And, more important, during this whole interval Buddhism
was to all intents and purposes unified.

While in the main following the period divisions given
above, some historians subdivide the earliest age into the
so-called period of original Buddhism and a subsequent
stage of primitive Buddhism. The basis for this subdivision
is the idea that in later times both understanding and expression of the Buddhism preached by Shakyamuni and his
direct disciples—that is, true original Buddhism—became
degraded and led in the direction of the formalism of sectarian Buddhism. This interpretation may be close to historical truth, though today, since it is possible to know of
presectarian Buddhism only from sectarian sources, there
is no documentary evidence for determining what is original Buddhism and what is primitive Buddhism. Scholars
and later sectarians speculate on the original form of Shakyamuni's teachings. But here I would like to dispense
with distinctions and consider all early Buddhist thought
as belonging to what is called primitive Buddhism.

The sectarian sources mentioned above are the Vinaya,
or precepts of the monastic order, and the oldest sutras, or
scriptures, preserved in the Pali and Chinese versions of
the Buddhist canon. Though they received their present

forms in the sectarian period and consequently reveal sectarian characteristics, clearly they all originated in the time of Shakyamuni. Furthermore, the essential position and ultimate goal of Buddhism as established by Shakyamuni are the same now as they were in his day, though over the centuries methods of interpreting the basic position have been transformed. In other words, a philosophical apparatus has been evolved to explain the essential teachings. Characteristically, Buddhism is open-minded on this point. Explanations may be freely devised or adjusted to suit the needs of the moment as long as they do not contradict or negate the Law.

Let us now briefly review the development of primitive Buddhism, beginning with the life of the Buddha himself. After renouncing his birthright as Prince Siddhartha Gautama (Pali, Siddhattha Gotama) of the Shakya tribe, Shakyamuni studied and practiced many of the philosophies and religions current in his time and found them all imperfect in one way or another. But after achieving complete enlightenment, he was able to reveal to the world a new set of logically sound, ethically pure, and universally applicable truths. As the Buddha, the Enlightened One, he was distressed by the spiritual confusion and moral decadence around him. Inspired by a sense of responsibility, he spent the rest of his life traveling around India preaching a message of deliverance from suffering. Shakyamuni did not venture far outside the central Ganges region, but several of his direct disciples who were from the distant reaches of western and southern India converted many people after returning to their homes. Even during the Buddha's lifetime, Buddhism advanced into the southwest, which was to become a great center of the faith after his death.

The Buddha died in Kushinagara at the age of eighty. Immediately afterward, the five hundred leading disciples (all *arhats,* or enlightened men) gathered together in the vicinity of Rajagriha to compile the teachings under the leadership of Maha-Kashyapa, one of the ten great disciples of the Buddha. Since there was no system of writing at the time, the compilation was oral. Ananda, the disciple who had heard more of the Buddha's sermons than anyone else, recited the Law—the Buddha's teachings—to the assembly. Upali, who kept the precepts best of all, recited the rules of conduct for the Buddhist community, the Order. The disciples present decided which of the sermons and precepts were to be included in the canon and then set about committing them to memory. This conference is known as the First Council, and the teachings collected there were divided into two categories, called *pitaka,* or baskets.

The memorized and orally transmitted teachings—the Law—later developed into the part of the canon called the Sutra-pitaka (Pali, Sutta-pitaka), the "sermon basket." The Sutta-pitaka of the Pali canon consists of five collections of sutras, called the Nikayas, and the Sutra-pitaka of the Chinese canon consists of four, called the Agamas. The precepts became the Vinaya-pitaka, the "precepts basket," which exists in several versions and contains both rules laid down by Shakyamuni for people who abandon secular life to become monks and stories relating how these precepts came into being. Though they occasionally record incidents after the Buddha's death, for the most part the Sutra- and Vinaya-pitaka pertain to his lifetime and are the prime historical sources for this period. The length of the interval between the First Council and the actual writing down of the canon is uncertain, as is the exact relation between the scriptures as they exist now and their earliest written versions. Nonetheless, the oldest forms of the Sutra-pitaka and Vinaya-pitaka are the primary sources for all modern studies of primitive Buddhism.

There is good reason to believe that in ages preceding the evolution of writing people were capable of feats of memory that seem impossible today. It is extremely unlikely, however, that even the talented Ananda and Upali had heard and remembered correctly all the Buddha's utterances. It is even less likely that their recitations at the First Council were handed down orally with complete accuracy until they could be recorded in script. It must be assumed, therefore, that the Buddhist scriptures are only imperfect reflections of the Buddha's actual words, which will probably never be known. Any attempt to reconstruct what the Buddha actually said on the basis of an assembly of the passages from his sermons that appear in all or most of the sectarian scriptures would be unsatisfactory, since not all sectarian versions of the teachings have survived.

Other factors complicate the situation. The Buddha taught in the local vernacular and insisted his disciples do the same. This meant that the teachings were often restated in different dialects in a process of translation that no doubt introduced alterations in both form and content. Divergence must have increased as distances separating Buddhist congregations grew too great to permit smooth, regular communication. Almost imperceptibly, the teachings and precepts must have been altered by differences in climate, geographic setting, and regional manners and mores until what had once been a single set of doctrines and commandments became a heterogeneous complex of sometimes mutually contradictory beliefs.

Even available historical documents fail to provide a full picture of the Buddha's original teachings because these writings are too much the product of a monastic tradition. It is perhaps understandable that during the age of sectarian Buddhism, when monasteries occupied a position of preeminence, monks had a strong influence on the content of the Vinaya-pitaka, which is, after all, a set of monastic ordinances. It is much less forgivable, however, that the monks failed to follow the Buddha's example of preaching to all people, monks and lay believers alike. From eighty to ninety percent of the sermons surviving in the early sutras are directed to monks. No doubt because in this period study and observance of the precepts took precedence over everything else and little effort was made to convey the teachings to ordinary people, many of the Buddha's sermons were neglected and have therefore been lost. Consequently, if the Buddha's true intent is to be discovered, surviving writings of early Buddhism must be subjected to close and critical scrutiny.

All of this perhaps inevitable divergence contributed to a conflict that arose a little more than a century after the Buddha's death and that was a sign of further troubles to come. The bone of contention was the precepts governing monastic life. Monks in the eastern district, near Vaishali, gave the rules a new interpretation that the conservatives in the west refused to accept. A conference of seven hundred elders—called the Second Council—convened at Vaishali ruled against the innovators and addressed itself to restating the traditional sutras and precepts.

Southern Buddhist sources report that the innovators broke away and formed a separate group at this time, giving some support to the idea that the Second Council was the scene of the initial schism. In contrast, the Northern Buddhist account says simply that a hundred or more years after the Buddha's death the followers split into conservative and revisionist factions over questions of doctrine, not discipline. There is no proof that these factions correspond to the sects of later history. Nonetheless, the passage of time and regional differentiation eventually led to the formation of two distinct branches of Buddhism: the conservative Theravada (Sthavira, or Teaching of the Elders) school in the south and the more innovative Mahasanghika (Great Assembly) school in the north.

SECTARIAN BUDDHISM

It is uncertain whether division into sects had actually taken place by 300 B.C., though, as I have said, the spread of the faith into various regions led to divergence that became a major cause of schism. Missionary efforts supported by the great Mauryan emperor Ashoka in the third century B.C. contributed to the religion's spread. Though the Pali tradition that eighteen or twenty sects existed during Ashoka's time is dubious, the very discrepancy between the Southern and Northern Buddhist accounts of Ashoka's life proves the existence of at least two groups ready to adopt different viewpoints. It is unclear whether the Third Council at Pataliputra, described in Pali texts as taking place during Ashoka's reign, was the scene of proliferating schism.

Before coming to the throne, Ashoka served for a number of years as governor-general in western India, living in Ujjeni, a center of Buddhist activity. There he may have heard of Buddhism for the first time, though he was prevented by a naturally violent and headstrong disposition from being converted. After the death of his father, Bindusara, Ashoka is said to have massacred his brothers, seized the throne, and proceeded to extend his empire in all directions, bringing the coastal district of Kalinga under his control in the eighth year of his reign. At this point, he seems to have undergone a change of heart. Tradition has it that remorse over the cruelty of the military campaign against Kalinga led him to accept Buddhism as his only hope of salvation.

Ashoka proved as ardent in faith as he had been in pursuit of power. He may even have become a monk for a time, though this point has been questioned. At any rate, he seems to have adopted the Buddhist view of the world and humanity, for he not only made Buddhism the court religion but also took steps to teach the Law at home and abroad. He is said to have built eighty-four thousand stupas and monasteries and to have succeeded in missionary efforts to make Buddhism an international, rather than a purely Indian, religion. Thanks, it is thought, to Ashoka's sponsorship of the faith, the Sarvastivada (Holders of the Doctrine That All Is) school of Buddhism took strong root in northwest India after the Third Council and the Theravada school of the south extended its influence to Sri Lanka. Knowledge of Buddhism was carried as far west as Greece and the areas under its control. Buddhist teachings may have left a mark on early Christianity, though no clear evidence has survived.

During the two or three centuries following Ashoka's reign, eighteen, twenty, or perhaps more Buddhist sects came into existence, marking the advent of what is called sectarian Buddhism. This subdivision of the religion, while having unfortunate aspects, testifies to great missionary and intellectual activity in the Buddhist world. Scholarly codification and explanation of scriptures, though pursued to some extent during the primitive period, attained full momentum during the age of the sects. Each sect devoted great effort to systematizing its creeds and devotional practices, as well as to clarifying philosophical concepts and terminology. This work went a long way toward providing Buddhism with both the theoretical foundation and the metaphysical systems that in a country like India, famed for speculative thought, must have been essential to survival.

Shakyamuni suited his sermons to the experience and intellectual capacity of his listeners, who differed widely in background. His aim was to tell all people how to find deliverance from suffering. Although he may have had a well-organized philosophical doctrine, he never burdened his audiences—at least his secular ones—with detailed exegesis or difficult metaphysical concepts. As recorded in the sutras, his sermons contain both the loftiest ideals and the most commonplace parables, but doctrines are presented only fragmentarily. To dedicated monks he stated his case in one fashion; with lay believers he adopted a less demanding style. His approach is reminiscent of that of an eloquent modern educator who effectively explains a theorem in one way to college students and in another to primary school pupils.

People who heard the Buddha's sermons were apparently able to grasp his meaning, but as time passed and the circumstances under which they had been delivered were forgotten, his sermons became increasingly difficult to understand fully. It was the task of later Buddhists to define obscure words, draw inferences, and pull everything together into an orderly system of belief. The resulting studies and expositions are called Abhidharma (Pali, Abhidhamma), or that which is "about the Law."

The origins of Abhidharma literature may be traced to the few works of explanation or commentary in the sutras of primitive Buddhism. In time, however, such expository writings became more specialized and detailed and diverged too far from the sutras to be included among them. Ultimately they came to constitute a distinct literary form occupying a separate division, or basket, in the canon, the Abhidharma-pitaka (Pali, Abhidhamma-pitaka). When this happened, the Tripitaka (Pali, Tipitaka), or Three Baskets— the sutras, the precepts, and the commentaries on the sutras—was complete.

Passed down (at least in theory) from the First Council, the sutras and precepts underwent no drastic alteration at the hands of the sects as they inevitably compiled their own versions of the scriptures. In the Abhidharma, however, sectarian distinctions assumed prominence. Indeed, these explanatory treatises are so characteristic of the period that its Buddhism is sometimes spoken of as Abhidharma Buddhism. The principal extant versions of the Buddhist canon of this period can be summarized briefly.

SUTTA-PITAKA. The Pali version of the sutras is a complete entity consisting of five collections:

1. Digha-nikaya (Long Discourses), containing 34 suttas

2. Majjhima-nikaya (Medium-length Discourses), containing 152 suttas
3. Samyutta-nikaya (Grouped Discourses), containing 56 groups of suttas
4. Anguttara-nikaya (Discourses Treating Enumerations), containing 11 groups of suttas
5. Khuddaka-nikaya (Minor Works), containing 15 suttas

The Agama Sutras, the Chinese versions of the oldest sutras, are composed of portions of works from four different schools. Fortunately, however, the four Agama sutras correspond closely to the first four sutra collections in the Pali canon:

1. Dirgha-agama (Long Discourses), containing 30 sutras of the Dharmaguptaka (Those Who Are Protected by the Law) school (22 fascicles)
2. Madhyama-agama (Medium-length Discourses), containing 222 sutras of a school in the Sarvastivada lineage (60 fascicles)
3. Samyukta-agama (Grouped Discourses), containing 1,362 sutras of the main Sarvastivada lineage (50 fascicles)
4. Ekottara-agama (Discourses Treating Enumerations), containing 481 sutras of an unidentified Mahayana school (51 fascicles)

The first Pali-Chinese pair contains longer sermons, the second medium-length sermons, and the third and fourth many short sermons. The fifth collection in the Pali Suttapitaka, the Khuddaka-nikaya, contains works that fit into none of the classifications of the first four and that vary widely in content and date of composition. The oldest seem to antedate the other collections of sutras and may already have existed during the Buddha's lifetime. Others are at least as old as the sutras in the other collections, and in some respects are even more important for the study of primitive Buddhism.

In addition to these complete works, there exist numerous fragments of independent sutras translated into Chinese, as well as a few Sanskrit fragments found in Chinese Turkestan and a number of brief works translated into Tibetan. The total quantity of all these fragments and short works, however, is minuscule in comparison with the Pali Sutta-pitaka.

VINAYA-PITAKA.   The extant integrated collections that are known as complete Vinaya are listed below. In addition, a number of fragmentary Vinaya texts survive in Chinese translations.

1. The Pali Vinaya, of the Theravada school
2. The Vinaya in Five Parts of the Mahishasaka school (30 fascicles)
3. The Vinaya in Four Parts of the Dharmaguptaka school (60 fascicles)
4. The Vinaya of the Mahasanghika school (40 fascicles)
5. The Ten-discourse Vinaya, sometimes called the Old Vinaya, of the Sarvastivada school (61 fascicles)
6. The New Vinaya of the Mula-Sarvastivada (Root Sarvastivadins) school (170 fascicles)
7. The Tibetan Vinaya, a complete translation of the original text of which the New Vinaya is a partial translation

The Pali Vinaya is representative of Vinaya texts. It contains three parts: the Sutta-vibhanga, the Khandhaka, and the Parivara. The Sutta-vibhanga is concerned primarily with basic prohibitions for monks and nuns, together with explanations of and commentaries on the rules. The Khandhaka deals with such ritual matters as the procedure for admission to the monkhood and the order of ceremony at the twice-monthly confessional as well as with rules for monastery life. The Khandhaka also includes regulations concerning food, clothing, everyday activities, and the mode of living to be followed during the annual retreats held during the three-month rainy season. The Parivara (or supplement) contains ancillary precepts.

While the Sutta-vibhanga and the Khandhaka are much the same for all schools, there is great variation among versions of the Parivara, which were no doubt composed after the rise of dissenting sects. Consequently, in order to understand the discipline as it was practiced in the primitive period, modern scholars must turn to the first two sections of the Vinaya.

ABHIDHARMA-PITAKA. Two Abhidharmas of seven works each survive from the sectarian period: the Pali Abhidhamma and, in Chinese translation, the Sarvastivada Abhidharma. The texts in the Pali and Sarvastivada Abhidharmas are historically classifiable as early, middle, and late. Early ones must have been compiled shortly after the first schism, since they are based on methods of exposition predating the formation of sects and reveal few sectarian distinctions. In the middle period, however, the sects had lost contact with one another, and the Abhidharmas differ considerably in subject matter and treatment. The late Abhidharmas, which vary so widely from sect to sect that they must be considered entirely independent works, were probably completed before the birth of Jesus. Also extant in Chinese translation is a single fascicle of the Shariputra Abhidharma, which may have been the Abhidharma of the Dharmaguptaka school. It dates mainly from the early and middle periods of the age of sectarian Buddhism.

The Pali Abhidhamma contains the following works:
1. Dhammasangani (Enumeration of Dhammas), an ethical analysis of the *dharmas,* experiential moments or mental states, early period
2. Vibhanga (Distinctions), doctrinal explanations followed by questions and answers, early period
3. Puggalapannatti (Description of Individuals), an analysis of personality types, early period

4. Kathavatthu (Subjects of Discussion), an orthodox polemical treatise, middle period
5. Dhatukatha (Discussion of Elements), an examination of the elements of existence, middle period
6. Yamaka (Book of Pairs), definitions of ambiguous terms, late period
7. Patthana (Book of Relations), a discussion of dependent origination, late period

The Sarvastivada Abhidharma contains:

1. Sangitiparyaya (Section for Recitation), an examination of doctrinal terms, early period
2. Dharmaskandha (Aggregate of Dharmas), a discussion of the stages of arhat practice, early period
3. Prajnapti (Book of Manifestation), cosmology and a discussion of psychological events, early period
4. Vijnanakaya (Group on Consciousness), a polemical treatise on the nonreality of the self, middle period
5. Dhatukaya (Group on Mental Elements), a psychological treatise, middle period
6. Prakaranapada (Treatise), an examination of the elements of existence, late period
7. Jnanaprasthana (The Course of Knowledge), definitions of key psychological terms and concepts, late period

Only the Pali Abhidhamma survives complete. Most of the Sarvastivada survives, though only in Chinese translation, and some portions have in fact been translated into Chinese at least twice. The Chinese translation of the Prajnapti is not complete, but a Tibetan version exists—the only portion of the Sarvastivada Abhidharma translated into Tibetan. Much of the Pali Abhidhamma has been translated into English, and all of it into Japanese.

Japanese scholars have pointed out that the same topics are treated in the Pali Vibhanga, the Sarvastivada Dharmaskandha, and the Chinese translation of the Shariputra Abhidharma. The Pali Puggalapannatti and the Shariputra

Abhidharma are also very similar. Western scholars had assumed that the Pali and Sarvastivada Abhidharmas were different versions of the same texts because of the great similarity in their titles, for example, the Dhatukatha (Pali) and the Dhatukaya (Sanskrit), but growing knowledge of the content of the Sarvastivada Abhidharma as preserved in the Chinese canon has resolved this misunderstanding.

A noncanonical but highly revered work of the second century B.C. deserves mention. Toward the middle of that century, a Greco-Bactrian king named Menander (Pali, Milinda) established a state in northwest India and apparently became a follower of the Buddha. The famous text called *Milindapanha* (The Questions of King Milinda), recording an erudite discussion of Buddhist principles that is supposed to have taken place between the monarch and the Buddhist priest Nagasena, allows us to draw a number of inferences about contemporary Buddhist thought.

EARLY MAHAYANA BUDDHISM

Sectarian Buddhism concerned itself first and foremost with strict observance of the monastic precepts and study of the scriptures, pursuits that encouraged dogmatism. Emphasis was on literal interpretation of the canon. In contrast, a group of pragmatic reformers, members of the Mahasanghika sect, favored interpreting the words of the scriptures in accord with their deeper meaning. Contending that many of the Buddha's important teachings had been either lost or ignored by literalists, the reformers regarded their more liberal approach as a way of reviving the founder's original intentions. Early Mahayana Buddhism developed out of this reformist movement within the Mahasanghika sect and was further influenced by the Dharmaguptaka school's emphasis on the veneration of stupas.

In the view of the Mahasanghika reformers, scholastically oriented Abhidharma Buddhism suffered from several flaws. Their arguments for reform can be summed up as follows.

While systematizing the teachings and clarifying certain concepts, Abhidharma Buddhism, the reformers claimed, tended to put everything on the same level and thus to obscure differences between genuine profundities and nonessentials. This could lead only to the debasement of the Buddha's loftier ideals, which in many cases failed to receive attention from sectarian scholars. By considering the teachings from one angle only, the monks who composed the Abhidharma writings had become excessively involved in ontological considerations, thus losing sight of the true meanings of the doctrines of the nonexistence of a persisting self and of *shunyata* (void or emptiness), which the Buddha had intended as rejections of theoretical metaphysics. In other words, Abhidharma thinkers attempted to analyze the phenomenal world as if it had inherent existence, though the Buddha had taught that all things are transient.

The reformers held that by overemphasizing questions of existence and karma (the results of actions, causality), the Abhidharma Buddhists had taken as their ideal an escapist nirvana without residue (emancipation from existence) divorced from the affairs of the world. This ran counter to the Buddha's message, reiterated throughout his long ministry, that all beings are interrelated and must therefore strive to save the world by saving one another. The Buddha's life—as well as his previous lives as a bodhisattva—had been single-mindedly oriented toward the salvation of others. He sought to achieve this goal, which is the bodhisattva ideal, by performing the six practices known as the Perfections (giving, observing the precepts, patience, striving, meditation, and wisdom) no matter what danger or discomfort this entailed. The Abhidharma Buddhists seemed to demonstrate a fear of suffering, while the ideal, manifested by the Buddha and the bodhisattvas, is obliviousness to suffering and lack of concern with one's own karma.

The reformers also criticized the religious ideal of sectarian Buddhism and claimed that the Abhidharma Buddhist *arhat* seeks to achieve only personal discipline and deliverance. In contrast, the bodhisattva works for the deliverance of all sentient beings. The excessive emphasis on study in Abhidharma Buddhism left no time to work for the betterment of society. In other words, Abhidharma Buddhism put too much emphasis on monastic life and too little on the activities of lay Buddhists.

The reformists believed that to correct these flaws it was necessary to reaffirm the original position of the Buddha by adopting the way of the bodhisattva instead of that of the *arhat*. Since they believed that the Buddhist philosophy they advocated was capable of transporting the entire sentient world to buddhahood, they called it Mahayana (the Great Vehicle) and disparagingly described Abhidharma Buddhism as Hinayana (the Small Vehicle).

Supported by new converts and by many Abhidharma Buddhists to whom the revisionist position appealed, Mahayana spread rapidly throughout India. At about the beginning of the first century A.D., scriptures based on Mahayana principles began appearing in a swelling stream that included a group of texts of various lengths called the Perfection of Wisdom sutras (*Prajnaparamita-sutras*), the Vimalakirti Sutra (*Vimalakirti-nirdesha-sutra*), the Flower Garland Sutra (*Avatamsaka-sutra*), the Lotus Sutra (*Saddharma-pundarika-sutra*), and the Amitabha Sutra (*Sukhavati-vyuha-sutra*), all destined to become great religious classics. Though these sutras are presented as having been preached by Shakyamuni himself, the oldest of them could have been written no earlier than about 450 years after his death. It is impossible to know who the authors were, but they were no doubt devout Buddhists convinced that their writings revealed the Buddha's true message.

The older Buddhist sects, stimulated by the Mahayana movement and striving to correct their deficiencies, continued to flourish until the early thirteenth century. Abhidharma study went forward unabated. The Sarvastivada school, the leading sect, was especially active in western India, where it produced many scholars who wrote numerous commentaries and treatises, one of the most outstanding of which was the two-hundred-volume Great Commentary (Abhidharma-mahavibhasha-shastra). In the long run, Mahayana insistence on the absence of a persisting self and on the doctrine of shunyata was to prevail over the Sarvastivada teaching that all things have substantial existence. Nonetheless, the Sarvastivada teachings, which the Mahayanists considered important fundamental introductory study material, exerted great influence on Hinayana and Mahayana sects alike. The attitude toward them was similar to the modern educational approach requiring elementary and secondary schooling as prerequisites to university study.

From documents setting forth the views of various sects and from Mahayana writings, it is evident that debate and conflict arose between the supporters of the older and newer forms of Buddhism. Yet dispute ended not in mutual destruction but in reflection and reform on both sides. The advent of several rival religions at about this time inspired all forms of Buddhism to cling together, thus sparing the Buddhist world the murderous sectarian rivalries that sundered Christianity.

The greatest exponent of early Mahayana Buddhism was Nagarjuna, who was active sometime between A.D. 150 and 250. In the Treatise on the Middle (Madhyamika-shastra), one of the earliest of his many writings, he set forth an extremely clear exposition of the absence of a self (atman) and the doctrine of shunyata as basic Buddhist tenets. Essentially a theoretical justification of the philosophy expressed in the Perfection of Wisdom sutras, this treatise became a cornerstone of Mahayana thought. Credited as the founder of eight sects, Nagarjuna was held in the highest esteem by Mahayana and Hinayana groups alike. In his writings and those of his disciple Aryadeva, early Mahayana philosophy achieved general completion by about 300.

In the second century A.D., northwest India was ruled by the Kushan tribes, whose most famous king, Kanishka (reigned c. 123–53), was a devout Buddhist. Under his aegis many Buddhist monasteries were erected, and Buddhist studies flourished as never before. Kanishka sponsored a great Buddhist council, the Fourth Council, where attending scholars wrote commentaries on the canon. The king later had these commentaries inscribed on copper plates and enshrined in a monument. Among the many priests and scholars who enjoyed his patronage, the most illustrious was Ashvaghosha, who, in addition to converting many people to Buddhism, was a poet and prolific author of such distinction that he is regarded by some as the founder of Indian musical drama.

Even before Kanishka's reign, northwest India had been the birthplace of the Gandhara school of Buddhist sculpture, which, influenced by Greek statuary, revolutionized Indian sculpture. Until the first century A.D., Indian Buddhists refrained from making images of the Buddha, choosing to represent him with such symbols as stylized renderings of his footprints, the Wheel of the Law, the bo tree under which he attained enlightenment, or a stupa containing his relics. By the time of the emergence of Gandhara and Mathura art (named for the central Indian kingdom of Mathura, where it originated), however, this restraint was abandoned, and a vast number of statues portraying not only Shakyamuni Buddha but also hosts of bodhisattvas and other buddhas were produced. Scholars differ on whether Gandhara or Mathura art came first, though Gandhara art is probably older. Both played a large role in the development of Gupta art, one of the glories of Indian civilization. Japanese sculpture of the seventh and eighth centuries, regarded by many as the finest produced in Japan, owes much to Gandhara art and later Indian antecedents.

MIDDLE-PERIOD MAHAYANA BUDDHISM

Early Mahayana was practical. It emphasized the salvation of ordinary people and strove to teach them how to realize the highest Buddhist ideals without worrying about philosophical problems. For instance, giving, the first of the Six Perfections, is something anyone can perform easily, as is chanting the name of Amitabha Buddha in the hope of rebirth in paradise after death, another practice taught in early Mahayana. People who carry out these practices can realize lofty Buddhist ideals in daily life without specialized learning or training because, early Mahayana Buddhism teaches, giving leads naturally to the attainment of enlightenment concerning the insubstantial nature of all things and because calling on Amitabha leads inevitably to indestructible, diamondlike faith.

Mahayana of the middle period, however, moved away from such religious practicality. Once the great early scriptures had gained currency and the religion had become established, Mahayana scholars, like the sectarian Buddhists before them, began to devote themselves to philosophical matters. This trend was stimulated in part by Hinayanists, whose speculative activities had gained new vigor, and in part by the non-Buddhist sects that formed what are known as the six systems of Indian philosophy. The influence of such activity prompted Mahayanists to take up scholarly study of their own doctrines. This trend marks the beginning of what is called middle-period Mahayana.

Sutras written after the time of Nagarjuna are concerned more with philosophical questions than with religious faith. Though evident even in the early Mahayana Flower Garland Sutra, this trend grew much more pronounced in the middle period, when three full-fledged philosophical systems developed: the philosophy of the buddha-nature (buddhagotra), the philosophy of the storehouse consciousness (alaya-vijnana), and a syncretic philosophy combining elements of the two.

The buddha-nature is the innate capacity enabling all who seek the ideal way to attain wisdom and nirvana. The concept developed from the Mahasanghika-school teaching that though chained to the cycle of transmigration by outside forces of ignorance and delusion, human nature is fundamentally pure. What Mahasanghika thinkers called a pure heart (or mind) was developed by Mahayana theorists into an all-encompassing buddha-nature. Storehouse consciousness means the totality of human mental and spiritual elements, including those accumulated in past existences. Sectarian thinkers had dealt with this topic in Abhidharma literature, though mainly in connection with superficial psychological phenomena operating in the outside world. In a more general sense, the storehouse consciousness is the accumulation of past experiences, which serves as a foundation for present spiritual and psychological activity and exerts great influence on superficial operations. In addition, it is the power that, by persisting, enables transmission of the karmic effects of present good and bad acts into future life. Buddha-nature deals with the essential nature of things, and the storehouse consciousness with their manifestations. The Mahayana idea of the buddha-nature evolved from Mahasanghika thought, while the concept of the storehouse consciousness derived from Abhidharma writings of the Theravada school.

Among the sutras setting forth the teachings of the buddha-nature, the best known are the Sutra of the Tathagata Treasury (Tathagatagarbha-sutra), the Sutra on That Which

Neither Increases Nor Decreases (*Pu-tseng pu-chien-ching*), the Queen of Shrimala Sutra (*Shrimaladevi-simhanada-sutra*), and the Mahayana Sutra of the Great Decease (*Mahaparinirvana-sutra*). Outstanding philosophical works, or *shastras* (treatises), on the subject include the Treatise on the Jewel-nature (*Ratnagotravibhaga-mahayanottaratantrashastra*) and the Treatise on the Buddha-nature (*Buddhagotra-shastra*). It is the Sutra of Profound Understanding (*Samdhinirmochana-sutra*) and, presumably, a no longer extant work called the Sutra on Mahayana Abhidharma (*Mahayana-abhidharma-sutra*) that explain the teaching of the storehouse consciousness. Leading philosophical treatises on the storehouse consciousness include the Treatise on the Stages of Yoga Practice (*Yogacharabhumi-shastra*) and the Treatise on the Establishment of the Doctrine of Consciousness Only (*Vijnaptimatratasiddhi-shastra*). The syncretic teaching combining the buddha-nature and the storehouse consciousness is found in the Sutra of the Appearance of the Good Doctrine in [Sri] Lanka (*Lankavatara-sutra*).

The school advocating the philosophy of the storehouse consciousness is called both the Consciousness Only (Vijnanavada) school and the Yogachara (Yoga Practice) school. Its philosophical system was perfected by Maitreyanatha (c. 270–c. 350) and by the brothers Asanga and Vasubandhu, active in the latter half of the fourth century. Although the syncretic school did not thrive in India, the Madhyamika (Middle Way) school, based principally on the writings of Nagarjuna and his disciple Aryadeva, and the Yogachara school were regarded as important by Buddhists and non-Buddhists alike. Equally valued were the Sarvastivada school and Sautrantika (literally, "sutra end") school, which broke away from the Sarvastivada school in the first century B.C. in disagreement with the parent group's excessive concentration on Abhidharma studies.

In the middle period of Mahayana development, the Sar-

vastivada school produced such important writings as the
Treatise on the Essence of Abhidharma (Abhidharma-
hridaya-shastra) by the third-century-A.D. writer Dharmashreshthin and the Expanded Treatise on the Essence of
Abhidharma (Samyuktabhidharma-hridaya-shastra) by the
fourth-century writer Dharmatrata. These works were expanded upon in the fourth century in Vasubandhu's Abhidharma Storehouse Treatise (Abhidharmakosha-shastra)
and in the fifth century in Samghabhadra's Treatise Following the True Teachings of the Abhidharma (Abhidharma-nyayanusara-shastra), both of which attracted great
attention in Indian scholarly circles. The principal work
on the Sautrantika school was the fourth-century writer
Harivarman's Treatise on the Completion of Truth (Satyasiddhi-shastra). The Yogachara school attempted to bring
all Buddhist philosophy together in a single system by in-
tegrating what it considered to be the superior elements of
Sarvastivada and Sautrantika thought with some of Nagarjuna's Mahayana theories.

It is generally thought that Mahayanists of the middle
period developed the most detailed and profound philosophical theories in all Buddhism, if not in the entire history of Indian thought. At this time, Buddhist scholars
even contributed to the theoretical study of principles of
logic. And though the Gupta court of the fourth and fifth
centuries favored the Brahmans, Buddhism continued to
command respect because of the steady stream of brilliant
philosophers it produced. It was partly because of Buddhist contributions that the Gupta period was a golden age
in art and letters as well as in philosophy and religion. One
aspect of the general cultural flowering was the adoption of
Sanskrit as the official language of the empire. It became
the language in which Buddhist scholars wrote, and Sanskrit translations were made of works that had earlier been
set down in a variety of local dialects.

The diaries of such Chinese monks as Fa-hsien (340?–

420?), Hsüan-tsang (c. 596–664), and I-ching (635–713), who journeyed to India in search of the Law, provide much information about Indian Buddhism of the period. Hsüan-tsang's diary is especially important because he traveled widely in India and wrote in great detail of what he saw. His journal makes it clear that in spite of the wide practice of Mahayana, Hinayana was superior in terms of numbers of monasteries and monks. His mention of regions in which Buddhism had almost disappeared reveals that in general it no longer flourished in India. The most powerful Hinayana sects were the regionally dominant Sarvastivada, Mahasanghika, and Theravada sects.

Hinayana overshadowed Mahayana at the time mainly because Mahayana had lost contact with the common people. Absorbed in philosophy and scholarship, its monks not only had neglected the practical aspects of religion but also had often ceased to abide by monastic discipline, thus demeaning themselves in the eyes of the laity. Then and in later times, Hinayana retained its strength because its priesthood held tenaciously to the monastic tradition and continued to serve as models of probity for lay believers.

LATE MAHAYANA BUDDHISM

Mahayana's excessive emphasis on scholarly questions with little meaning in terms of practical faith can only be viewed as a sign of deterioration. In the seventh and eighth centuries, as if to recapture earlier vitality and appeal, Vajrayana (the Thunderbolt Vehicle), or Tantric, Buddhism appeared. While preserving the philosophical systems of earlier Mahayana, Tantric Buddhism tried to express philosophic truth symbolically and thus to make religious implications simple enough for anyone to understand.

Graphic representations of the Buddhist universe called mandalas were used to explain difficult doctrines. Believers were told they could achieve buddhahood by performing magic rites and repeating the mantras, or true words, of certain buddhas and bodhisattvas; by contemplating the sacred letters supposed to characterize those buddhas and bodhisattvas; and by employing mystical hand positions, or mudras. In addition to the Diamond Peak Sutra (*Vajrashekhara-sutra*) and the Great Sun Sutra (*Mahavairochana-sutra*), Tantric Buddhism reveres a large number of ritual manuals setting down the mantras and the proper ways of worshiping various beings.

For two or three hundred years, beginning around the middle of the eighth century, Tantric Buddhism flourished in east-central India under the auspices of the Pala dynasty. It tended, however, to become confused with if not actually incorporated into popular Hinduism—which is not surprising, since Hinduism was the original source of the Tantric elements in this branch of Buddhism. Gradually the true spirit of the Buddha disappeared from Indian Buddhism, to be replaced by the vulgar, often lascivious, hedonism of what is called left-hand Tantrism, or Shaktism.

Weakened from within, Buddhism was also attacked from without. In the eighth century, while adopting many of the superior features of Buddhist philosophy, orthodox Brahmans lured Buddhists away from their faith with a new, more elevated form of Hinduism, which subsequently became the national faith of most of India. Simultaneously, fanatic Muslims, infiltrating from the northwest, attacked and destroyed many Buddhist monasteries in the course of their campaign against idolatry. By this time, Buddhist establishments in general no longer turned to the common people for alms, since they could rely on their own lands for economic sustenance. Such financial independence no doubt contributed to the monks' aloofness from the religious needs of the laity. By turning away from the people, the Buddhist establishments deprived themselves of wide popular support and made themselves especially vulnerable to the destructive raids of the Muslims. The Buddhist faith was gone; only monasteries and monks remained. When these were wiped out, Buddhism ceased to exist in India. The obliteration was complete by the year 1200.

In Sri Lanka, however, where it had been carried during the reign of Ashoka, Theravada Buddhism continued to thrive, and it later spread to Burma, Thailand, Cambodia, and Laos, which remain strongholds of Southern Buddhism today. Roughly at the beginning of the first century A.D., the Buddhism of northwest India spread through Central Asia to China, where for more than a millennium it remained an important religious and intellectual force, nourished by frequent infusions of Hinayana and Mahayana thought via both the northern land and the southern sea routes. Chinese Buddhism in turn was carried to Korea and Japan, where it constituted a vital civilizing force. Today, Northern Buddhism, as preserved in East Asian nations, is the second great branch of the faith.

In the seventh century, middle and late Mahayana Buddhism traveled to Tibet, where it continued to grow under direct Indian influence until Buddhism in India collapsed completely. The presence in Tibet of many Mahayana scriptures that never reached China gives Tibetan Buddhism an aspect quite different from the Buddhism of either East Asia or Southeast Asia. Though failing to survive in the land of its birth—as Christianity has largely failed to survive in the Middle East—Buddhism has passed into many foreign lands through its scriptures, to become an object of both scholarly research and faith for millions of people throughout southern and eastern Asia.

2 The Fundamentals of Shakyamuni's Philosophy

THE THREE TREASURES

Faith in the Three Treasures—the Buddha, the Law, and the Order—has been the religious characteristic of all Buddhism, Hinayana or Mahayana, throughout the twenty-five hundred years of its history. Some Western scholars have argued that because it has no deity Shakyamuni's Buddhism is not a religion but a system of ethics, morality, and philosophy. But such scholars overlook the religious nature of faith in the Three Treasures.

If Buddhism were no more than a philosophical and ethical system, it would not have survived to this day as the faith of billions of people. Profound and diligent study of Buddhist philosophy can make a Buddhologist but not a Buddhist. Today, as in Shakyamuni's time, being a Buddhist means having religious faith in the Three Treasures. The formula "I take refuge in Gautama the World-honored One, in the Law, and in the Order of Monks. World-honored One, from this day to the end of my life, recognize me as a believer who has taken refuge" occurs time and again in the earliest Buddhist scriptures and means that even without theoretical understanding, a person who has faith in the Three Treasures is a true Buddhist.

39

I do not intend to go into the various interpretations of the Three Treasures advanced by scholars. The Japanese Zen priest Dogen (1200–1253) spoke for Buddhists of all time when he said, "We take refuge in the Buddha because he is our great teacher; in the Law, because it is good medicine; and in the Order, because it is composed of excellent friends." Set phrases of similar meaning occur frequently in primitive Buddhist texts.

The Buddha deserves to be revered because he is the founder of the faith, the source of the teachings, and the greatest human being who ever lived. Reading the sutras and studying the teachings only increase awareness of his greatness. The Law deserves to be revered because it was discovered and preached by the Buddha and because it heals the spirit, just as effective medicines heal the body. Like a great doctor, the Buddha always selected the best remedy for the illness of the moment. His remedy was a truth that is universally applicable to all people in all times. The Order is composed of friends who guide the believer in faith. After Shakyamuni's death, it became the responsibility of the priesthood to propagate the faith, offer salvation to the masses, and protect and preserve the teachings. Through the efforts of the Order, the Law spread and survived, and for this reason Buddhist priests have been regarded as the treasures of the nations in which they have lived. It is the duty of the Order to interpret the Law correctly and enable it to serve as a good remedy. Whether its members are outstanding determines whether Buddhism flourishes or fails. This is why the Order must be of a caliber to warrant the kind of absolute faith afforded to the Buddha and the Law.

The four indestructible objects of faith in which true believers put unshakable trust are the Three Treasures (Buddha, Law, and Order) and the precepts (not to kill, not to steal, not to indulge in wrong sexual activity, not to lie, not to drink intoxicants). The person who profoundly believes in the Three Treasures will abide absolutely by these moral rules. The aim of Buddhism is for believers of this kind to convert the world into a place of peace and happiness free of war, strife, antagonism, envy, injustice, and iniquity.

BUDDHISM AS PHILOSOPHY

For the ordinary lay person, Shakyamuni urged simple belief in the Three Treasures and adherence to fundamental moral precepts—devotion to the four indestructible objects of faith, which eliminate the temptation to be attracted by false creeds and lead without fail to enlightenment. In other words, people with faith can make Buddhism their own through experience even when they lack thorough knowledge of Buddhist philosophy. Nonetheless, anyone who wishes to understand the ultimate truth of Buddhism and to grasp fully its view of the world and humankind must study Buddhist philosophy. This is especially true for members of the Order, who are specialists required to guide ordinary people in their faith, answer questions, and quell doubts.

Three teachings are found in primitive Buddhist texts as explanations of the nature of the Law and the fundamental doctrines of Buddhism: the Buddhist law of causation, or, more specifically, the law of dependent origination (pratitya-samutpada), the seals of the Law, and the Four Noble Truths (arya satyas). The first occupies a position of central importance and is indeed the nucleus of all Buddhist philosophy. The law of dependent origination and Buddhism are identical. The Buddha said, "The person who understands the Law understands dependent origination, and the person who understands dependent origination understands the Law."

Fundamental to the law of dependent origination are the seals (or marks) of the Law. Seal is used in the sense of a brand that guarantees the validity of a document and serves as a person's mark. Thus the seals of the Law are simultaneously its characteristics and its proof. Any theory that conforms to these characteristics is true; any theory that fails to do so is false. The three seals state that all things are impermanent, nothing has a persisting self, and nirvana is tranquillity. Sometimes a fourth, all existence is suffering, is added to make the four seals of the Law.

The Four Noble Truths, a kind of simplified law of causation, are perhaps the best known of all the Buddha's teachings: all existence is suffering, the cause of suffering is craving and illusion, suffering can be eliminated, and the way to eliminate suffering is to follow the Eightfold Path (ashtangika-marga) consisting of right views, right thought, right speech, right action, right livelihood, right effort, right mindfulness, and right meditation. As if to indicate their importance, Shakyamuni took the Four Noble Truths and the Eightfold Path as the subjects of his very first sermon, celebrated as "setting the Wheel of the Law in motion," delivered to five ascetics at Deer Park near Benares.

Since the law of dependent origination, the Four Noble Truths, and the seals of the Law—the fundamental teachings of primitive Buddhism—are essentially the same, theoretically it would be possible to cover them all by explaining only one. But for the sake of clarity I shall deal with them separately, though in a related fashion. Before proceeding to specifics, however, it is essential to explain the general viewpoint from which the Buddha's Law developed. It is not philosophical theory for its own sake but theory intended to serve as the foundation of the practice of religious faith. Buddhism calls everything that is unrelated to religion empty debate (prapancha) and insists that all theory be useful in human life, relieve suffering, and turn human beings in the direction of the ideal. At the same time, theory must not conflict with scientific fact or moral justice or it runs the risk of becoming either superstition or evil doctrine. Shakyamuni himself frequently said that religious doctrine must be not only true and correct but also useful.

Since Buddhism rejects as harmful all ontological or metaphysical exegesis that is unrelated to religious experience, its philosophy is unconcerned with what exists and how it exists. In Shakyamuni's own time, many philosophers and men of religion expended great time and effort trying to decide whether the world of spirits and gods actually exists and, if it exists, whether it is subject to limitation. The Buddha, however, perceived that if there is indeed an ultimate ontological reality, it must transcend time and space and consequently be so far beyond our experience that we lack the intellectual capacity to recognize it. He saw that arguments about existence and nonexistence are meaningless and that any theoretical conclusions arrived at in connection with such topics are irrelevant to the world of human experience and therefore useless as a key to the problems of human life and suffering. Rejecting idle speculation, Shakyamuni was concerned (as all Buddhists must be) with the present life, its joys, sorrows, loves, hates, and infinite choices. In other words, instead of being concerned with existence as an abstract study, Buddhist philosophy deals with the nature of the human condition in this life and the manner in which human beings respond to it.

This is not to say that Buddhist philosophy ignores ontological considerations. On the contrary, it both recognizes phenomenal, or common-sense, existence and regards the definition and description of such existence as its proper field of study. The theory of the five aggregates (skandhas), for example, which explains human beings as a compound of physical and mental aspects and further divides the mental aspect into feeling, perception, dispositions, and consciousness, is an ontological Buddhist concept but remains based on life as human beings live it

rather than life as an abstract concept. Buddhist episte-
mological concepts, such as the twelve sense-fields, deal
with the ways in which the senses and intellect confront
everyday occurrences. All of these doctrines attempt to
answer questions, not of pure existence but of the real nature of the phenomena of actual experience and the ways
human beings deal and cope with them. It is, accord-
ingly, of prime importance to state clearly that the three
(or four) seals of the Law deal not with whether existence
itself exists but with the actual and optimum natures of existence. Unless this is fully understood, it is possible to
misinterpret the concepts of absence of self and *shunyata*
as nihilistic when, in fact, they were devised precisely to
refute nihilism.

THE SEALS OF THE LAW

In the first seal of the Law, all things are impermanent, "all
things" means all physical and mental phenomena. Everything is constantly changing, and Shakyamuni made this
statement of the ephemeral nature of all things first as a
fact that people must experience in daily life. Clearly the
operations of the mind are fluid, but even such apparently
stable objects as rocks and trees are constantly undergoing
change. From the minutest physical particles to the largest
celestial bodies, nothing ceases to move for a moment.
Modern scientific theories about this kind of flux make it
easier than in the past to accept the idea that all things are
impermanent.

One of Shakyamuni's purposes in teaching the law of
universal impermanence was to enable human beings to
see the world as a complex of phenomena instead of as an
ultimate reality with a permanent, unalterable nature. Another purpose was to lay a foundation for the second seal
of the Law: nothing has a persisting self. Primitive Buddhist scriptures often say that the five aggregates—that is,

the elements of which all sentient beings are composed—
are the source of suffering because they are impermanent
and therefore have no lasting self. But it would be wrong to
assume that sorrow is the only consequence of impermanence; in fact, it has several fortunate implications. It
frees human beings from pride and attachment to the
things of this world. It provides courage to face destiny
without discouragement. And it makes possible a total concentration of energy on the present.

Pessimistic connotations attached to words like impermanence and transience lead people to dwell on the negative side of this doctrine and to think that impermanence
means only that the mighty fall and that health gives way
to sickness. But change does not always mean change for
the worse. The humble are often raised, and the sick
made well. Poverty is no less impermanent than riches,
foolishness no less fleeting than wisdom. Misery can
change to joy, and a sinner can become a saint. Buddhism
teaches impermanence in order to change suffering to joy,
misery to happiness, and the ordinary mortal to a sage, and
to show that all things and all people can alter. In this way
it offers the hope and courage needed to face destiny without despair.

Despite the truth that nothing is permanent, many people
pridefully regard their youth, health, wealth, and position
as immutable and hope to enjoy these blessings eternally.
But all these things must inevitably alter; the teaching of
universal impermanence helps human beings be modest
about their advantages and avoid pride in and attachment
to any of them. Since all things change from instant to instant, life is an accumulation of momentary actions and hap-
penings. Each of these moments must be fulfilled, not with
carpe diem hedonism but with a provident realization of
the individual's full potential.

"Nothing has a persisting self" means that there is no
essential or permanent being; nothing that does not come

into being, change, and eventually pass out of being; nothing that exists of itself, without relation to other beings. Everything is constantly being transformed. All things are related in some way to all other things in the universe. Furthermore, there is no fixed reality behind the generation, change, and destruction of phenomena.

In the India of Shakyamuni's day, some philosophers claimed that human beings and their behavior are controlled by the will of a god or by immutable fate. But if everything moves in accordance with the will of an omnipotent god, the creator and ruler of the earth, there is no free will. Consequently, human beings are unable to change fate through the exercise of will or physical effort. All attempts at self-improvement are futile. Carried to its logical conclusion, this theory leaves no room for education, which aims at the betterment of society, or for religion, which strives for deliverance from sorrow. Humanity has no choice but to accept whatever comes.

The fatalists of Shakyamuni's day taught that at birth each individual is fated—whether by karma or, as some schools insisted, by the effects of the four elements of water, fire, earth, and air—to live with a set of circumstances that cannot be altered. Free will has no place in deterministic systems of this kind; therefore, self-discipline, education, and religion are meaningless. According to Marxist dialectical materialism, a modern form of predestination, society is bound to develop in conformity with certain economic determinants. This line of thought goes back to Hegelian dialectic, which is deterministic in its suggestion that society and human life must proceed along a fixed course. From the Buddhist viewpoint, Hegelian philosophy is objectionable because it assumes the existence of an absolute higher spirit. The ultimate import of Marxist dialectic is so inhospitable to any hope for social betterment that it has been soft-pedaled, if not actually repudiated, by most communists.

Various terms were used at different times to indicate the meaning of the second seal of the Law: in Sanskrit, *anatman* (devoid of self) in primitive Buddhist scriptures and *shunyata* (void, emptiness) in Mahayana texts; and in Chinese, by the Zen Buddhists, *wu* (not). But all of these terms mean the absence of any fixed self or permanent nature, not utter nonexistence. The second seal of the Law expresses the ultimate goal of Buddhism as the attainment of the state in which realization of the impermanence and transience of all things liberates human beings from attachments of all kinds and enables them to act free and unhindered in accordance with the Law.

The Buddhist law of dependent origination is the logical integration of the first two seals of the Law. In simple terms, dependent origination means that every effect has a definite cause and every cause a definite effect. Nothing comes into being by accident. Actions do not occur in a haphazard fashion. Only when certain causes and conditions are present can a particular effect or result be achieved. This is by no means to imply an all-encompassing first cause like divine will or a foreordained plan for life. Causes and conditions vary in infinite ways to generate infinite kinds of results. But for any fixed set of causes and conditions, the result, too, is fixed.

The law of dependent origination analyzes life and the workings of human beings and society as they actually are. In Shakyamuni's day, other philosophies were much less objective. Theories of an omnipotent deity and deterministic and accidentalist teachings violated the law of cause and effect and advocated futile, if not downright pernicious, religious practices. For instance, people were told they could achieve enlightenment by fasting and asceticism, that imitating the actions of such animals as dogs and elephants was the path to rebirth in paradise, or that bathing in certain rivers could cleanse the soul and wash away sins. But the Buddha saw that these doctrines and practices defied reason, since it cannot be shown that mortification of the flesh is the cause of enlightenment, that mimicking animals is the cause of rebirth in bliss, or that washing in a river is spiritually purifying.

The correct Buddhist view of the world and humankind is inseparable from the law of dependent origination. In symbolizing this relationship, primitive Buddhist texts describe an aspirant who has acquired proper understanding and has arrived at the first stage of enlightenment as having received the Eye of the Law, unblemished and unsoiled. Frequently, similar texts say that the Eye of the Law consists in being able to see that all things born of causes and conditions cease to exist when those causes and conditions are destroyed. In short, a person who has attained this stage of understanding perceives the principle of dependent origination, equated with the immutable Law.

Dependent origination, founded on the principles of impermanence and lack of a persisting self, is purely neutral, involving no value judgments. In real life, however, everything is subject to a value judgment of some kind: things are pleasant or painful, good or evil, sacred or profane. The final two seals of the Law—all existence is suffering and nirvana is tranquillity—provide the value foundation for the law of dependent origination, of cause and effect.

Everyone is aware of the physical suffering of illness or privation and the spiritual suffering of frustration or the fear of death. But life also has undeniable pleasures: riches, good health, the joy of satisfying deep desires, and even, for some, the welcome relief of death. For saying that all existence is suffering, Buddhism has been criticized as pessimistic and has been branded gloomy and otherworldly by some Western thinkers. Such criticism, however, mistakes the true meaning of the statement that all existence is suffering and ignores its connection with nirvana as tranquillity. Buddhism calls attention to the burdens of life in order to lay the groundwork for the message that there is a way out. Anyone who sees only the truth of suffering and fails to see the truth of the extinction of suffering misses the point completely.

The higher a person's ideals, the greater his or her disappointment with the imperfections, insufficiencies, and hardships of the world. In comparison with visions of perfection, life is a vale of tears. But awareness of life's imperfections leads human beings to religion as the sole path to deliverance and salvation. If life were free of sorrow and anxiety and filled with nothing but joy and happiness, there would be no need for religion or faith. Recognition of life's sorrows and of individual foibles and pain is where religion begins. The statement that all existence is suffering is the gateway to the Buddhist faith and the only possible view of the unenlightened present for an unenlightened human being.

No more permanent than any other aspect of the world, suffering can be converted into happiness. But seeking the reason for suffering's existence is the necessary first step toward achieving this transformation. Only by examining the causal relationship giving rise to sorrows is it possible to discover a logical way to eliminate them. Shakyamuni did precisely this. The second of the Four Noble Truths gives the cause of suffering as craving. (The Twelve-linked Chain of Dependent Origination, discussed in chapter three, is a more detailed explanation of the cause of suffering.) The third and fourth Noble Truths enunciate the way to eliminate suffering, testifying to a state in which suffering is extinct and teaching the Eightfold Path as the way to reach that state. Thus we see the close interrelation of the seals of the Law, the Four Noble Truths, and the law of dependent origination.

The principles of universal impermanence and the lack of a persisting self underlie the neutral law of dependent origination, which is unconcerned with human values. The doctrines of universal suffering and nirvana are the foundation for practical application of the law of dependent origination in which value judgment is implicit. In other words, the law of dependent origination serves as the supporting framework for the Four Noble Truths.

VIEWS OF HUMANKIND AND FATE

The philosophy of Buddhism inevitably fell under the direct or indirect influences of other schools of thought prevalent in the India of the Buddha's day. Nothing can occur without relation to its historical environment, but great teachers like the Buddha can rise above that environment and create one of their own. Shakyamuni thoroughly examined all the philosophical and religious doctrines of his time. Adopting what he found worthwhile and discarding what he found useless, he established the Buddhist philosophy, which is distinguished from all others by its teaching of dependent origination, a teaching the Buddha himself described as an unprecedented but absolute truth, universally applicable. The following chapter treats the Twelve-linked Chain of Dependent Origination in detail. For the purposes of the general discussion here, suffice it to say that the central concept on which it is based is that all phenomena are produced by causation and are therefore neither spontaneous nor fortuitous.

This doctrine differs from all its contemporaries in its goal. The other philosophies of ancient India attempted to examine the question of ultimate and original existence, while the Buddha insisted that such things lie in a realm beyond human experience and comprehension. A common-sense religion, Buddhism is concerned first not with abstracts beyond human ken but with the world of actual experience and with enabling human beings to live well in it. To this end the Buddha presented the teachings of the seals of the Law, dependent origination, and the Four Noble Truths.

A number of Shakyamuni's contemporaries strongly opposed the idea of dependent origination and karmic causation. Various schools of thought interpreted fate and humankind's role in the world and society in different ways. For some, everything was determined by divine will. The orthodox Brahman believed that the creator gods Brahma and Maheshvara control everything in the universe, including human actions and behavior. To obtain blessings from the gods it was essential to pray, make sacrifices, and perform other acts of propitiation. Subscribers to this view resorted to slaughtering other living creatures to provide the sacrifices they hoped would bring them divine blessings. But perhaps the most serious shortcoming of belief in the omnipotent will of a divinity is the effect it has on human efforts at self-discipline and development. If all is in the hands of the gods, such effort is fruitless and meaningless.

Several other prominent approaches to humankind and fate were current in the Buddha's time. Some taught a relentless fatalism, holding that everything is inexorably determined by karma from past existences and cannot be altered in the slightest. This approach has as debilitating an effect on human effort as does belief in omnipotent divine will. Another leading philosophy of the time was the belief in innate class position. According to this doctrine, human beings are born into one of six classes that inexorably determine for all time social position, circumstances, life span, intellectual capacities, physical strength, and so on. Yet another teaching, the doctrine of constituent elements, held that a person's fate is governed entirely by the way the four elements combined at his or her birth. In some respects similar to modern beliefs that blood type or genetic inheritance determines everything in life, this philosophy fails to take into consideration causes and conditions other than the four elements and is therefore another brand of fatalism.

None of these philosophies leaves any room for self-improvement for the sake of altering one's fate. Under these systems, education, self-discipline, and religious training with the goal of self-perfection are meaningless and valueless. They all contrast greatly with Buddhism, which, while adopting the idea of causal relations and karma from general Indian philosophy, assumes the possibility of altering fate and personality by adding good or bad karma during one's lifetime.

Still, all of those systems posit causation of one kind or another. Others who philosophized about the human situation in the Buddha's day rejected all cause, direct or indirect, and insisted that everything occurs spontaneously and accidentally. Shakyamuni's was a time of strife and turmoil. Often the good suffered and the evil flourished, and it was difficult for some people to believe in either causal determination or divine will. Under such conditions, people understandably failed to see cause in anything and consequently espoused a hedonistic philosophy.

All the doctrines outlined so far fall well within the confines of orthodox Indian thought and religion. During Shakyamuni's day, however, many unorthodox men of religion sought truth in their own ways. Shakyamuni was one of them. Several of his contemporaries and near-contemporaries are referred to in Buddhist texts as the six heterodox (that is, non-Buddhist) teachers. The philosophies of these men, while distinct in many respects, partially resemble more orthodox views but generally differ strongly from the down-to-earth, practical moral orientation of Buddhism.

Purana-Kassapa, one of these six men, flatly rejected the idea of causation. In the Pali Sutra on the Fruits of the Life of a Recluse (*Samannaphala-sutta*), he is reported to have declared that a person's merit neither increases nor decreases, no matter what amount of wickedness, including the mutilation and slaying of multitudes of people, or what amount of good, including alms giving and sacrifices, that person may accomplish. Makkhali-Gosala, another of the six heterodox teachers, was originally a Jainist and a disciple of Mahavira, the founder of Jainism, but later developed his own philosophy. Makkhali-Gosala denied all causes, ultimate, proximate, and remote, and insisted that the class into which living creatures are born determines their good or bad fortune, which neither industry nor lethargy on their part can alter.

The materialist Ajita-Kesakambali also repudiated cause and effect, insisting that human beings are constituted solely of earth, water, fire, and air and disappear entirely at death, leaving behind nothing for karma to affect. Since, according to him, the elements that had been compounded during the human being's life revert to their original state at death, it is foolish to speak of the good and bad karma of compassionate or wicked acts. Interestingly, materialism—exemplified by the teachings of the Carvaka, or Lokayata, school—continued to influence Indian thought long after Ajita-Kesakambali. While rejecting religion and morality, however, Indian materialists usually engaged in self-disciplinary and ascetic practices, perhaps as a criticism of the hypocritical men of religion they saw around them.

The atomist Pakudha-Kacchayana posited seven permanent, immutable categories (earth, water, fire, air, ease, pain, and the soul), which can be neither created nor formed, and insisted that since these categories do not violate, harm, or in any way affect one another, no actor or acted-upon exists. There can be no slayer and no slain; no one hears and no one causes to hear; no one knows or causes to know. When one man strikes another with a sword, he does not inflict the wound himself; the weapon merely passes through the elements of the victim's body.

These philosophers rejected out of hand the idea of karma. The skeptic Sanjaya-Belatthiputta neither accepted nor rejected it, because he felt that there can be no abso-

lute knowledge about anything. He believed that since it is
unthinkable that a single issue can be interpreted in many
different ways, the various doctrines about humankind and
fate propounded by the teachers of the time were totally
subjective. Sanjaya-Belatthiputta considered it wiser to
stop squabbling over whose interpretation of good and bad
was right and to follow a course of serious, practical action. Though it may be well motivated from the theoretical
and scholarly viewpoints, such skepticism stops short of a
thorough examination of the issue and is somewhat
cowardly. Skeptics who doubt everything are ultimately
reduced to the embarrassing position of being forced to
doubt their own teachings as well. From the Buddhist viewpoint, this philosophy is sophistic. (Two of the Buddha's
leading disciples, Shariputra and Maudgalyayana, were
followers of Sanjaya-Belatthiputta at one time but became
dissatisfied with his teachings and became Buddhists on
hearing Shakyamuni's teachings. Shariputra's uncle,
known as "the itinerant ascetic with the long fingernails,"
became a Buddhist after being shown the contradictions in
the skeptic doctrines he too had embraced till then.)

The last of the six heterodox teachers was Mahavira, the
founder of Jainism. It is probably because Mahavira accepted and adopted the doctrines of causation and karmic
retribution common in his time that Jainism grew vigor-
ously—second only to Buddhism itself—and has persisted
to the present, with more than two million followers in
India today. From the Buddhist standpoint, the Jainists are
fatalists in theory, though they are much less so in practice.
Their seriousness has won them the trust and respect of
many people who do not share their views.

CAUSATION

Buddhist thought rejected all of these philosophical approaches and many other current superstitious views on

discipline and fate as misinterpretations of the true relationship between cause and effect and made correcting
them one of its aims. Two factors distinguish dependent
origination, the Buddhist doctrine of causation, from contemporary Indian philosophies. First, it confines itself to
the world of actual experience and makes no attempt to
deal with universal absolutes, which are beyond the realm
of human cognizance and influence. Second, while teaching that given the requisite conditions each cause produces
its inevitable effect, it rejects both the idea that human fate
is fortuitous and the idea that it is completely governed by
any single, fixed cause.

Despite correspondences between the law of dependent
origination and the facts of modern science, Buddhism
deals not with science and reason but with the cause of suffering in human life and the way to eliminate it and make
possible the attainment of an ideal state. In primitive Buddhist thought, the principles behind the theory are set forth
in various concrete forms. One of the best known is the
Twelve-linked Chain of Dependent Origination. In addition to this doctrine, there occur such formulaic descriptions as "If this exists, that exists; if this comes into being,
that comes into being; if this is not, that is not; if this ceases
to be, that ceases to be"; or "All things that come into being
must pass out of being"; and of course the Four Noble
Truths, which, though oriented toward training and self-
discipline, take the form of a causal explanation. All of
these expressions of the theory are fundamental and stand-
ardized and do not deal with particular phenomena.

In the history of Buddhism, two main opinions as to the
nature of cause-and-effect relations have evolved. Sectarian Buddhism first devoted more attention to relations
between causes and effects: the cause-and-effect relations
of time and space, nature, directness and indirectness,
simultaneous and parallel action, dependence, positive-
ness and negativeness, and so on. The essence of these

subtle categorizations and analyses, however, is that all phenomena are intimately related to all others through cause and effect. In terms used by such later Chinese schools of Buddhism as Hua-yen (Flower Garland), "One is all and all is one."

The doctrine of dependent origination found in Theravada and sectarian Buddhism and in the teachings of later schools of East Asian Buddhism emphasizes the sequential time relationship with regard to karmic effects. According to this view, cause necessarily precedes effect. The second interpretation is found in the teachings of the Perfection of Wisdom sutras; Indian Madhyamika Buddhism and its Chinese incarnation, the San-lun (Three Treatises) school; and the T'ien-t'ai school, whose doctrines are derived from the Lotus Sutra. This interpretation insists that all causes and effects exist simultaneously and likens their influence on one another to spatial relations rather than to time sequence. Although the two interpretations seem separate and exclusive, in fact each includes elements of the other, since dependent origination describes all things in both time and space.

Various interpretations of the doctrine of dependent origination are possible. For instance, dependent origination can be thought of as an eternal principle or as an explanation of the phenomena and events of actual life. Shakyamuni declared that dependent origination is an eternal truth, whether or not buddhas appear on earth to proclaim it. In addition, however, he dealt with dependent origination in the emerging, changing, and disappearing phenomena of daily life. A similar distinction between abstract, theoretical interpretations and actual, practical interpretations may be made in connection with the Four Noble Truths and with various elements of Buddhist philosophy and faith.

Dependent origination can be analyzed in terms of internal, psychological and external, objective effects. But in all its interpretations, dependent origination is either general and neutral or value oriented. Neutral dependent origination is of the kind expressed in such formulas as "If this exists, that exists; if this comes into being, that comes into being; if this does not exist, that does not exist; and if this ceases to exist, that ceases to exist." In contrast to the doctrine of neutral dependent origination, which merely explains how things come into and go out of being, the value-oriented teaching of dependent origination teaches human beings how to do something about the objective situation explained by neutral dependent origination. The values to which this type of dependent origination is applied are the Buddhist values of good and evil, purity and defilement, enlightenment and delusion, not the limited rational values of true and false. Value-oriented dependent origination includes the teaching that ignorance, the first link of the Twelve-linked Chain, ultimately leads to birth, aging, death, and rebirth, that is, to bondage within the cycle of transmigration. It also includes the teaching that escape from that cycle and the attainment of an ideal state are possible if first ignorance and then all the other links in the chain are eliminated

No matter how it is interpreted and applied, the law of dependent origination has remained the essence of all Buddhism from the primitive teachings through the Theravada and sectarian Abhidharma systems to the Mahayana teachings as they evolved in India, China, and Japan. In the Greater Discourse on the Simile of the Elephant's Footprint (Mahahatthipadopama-sutta), a Pali text, Shakyamuni states, "The person who understands dependent origination understands the Law, and the person who understands the Law understands dependent origination." In the system of Buddhist practice, the practitioner who has come to understand the most fundamental expression of the law of dependent origination, "All things that come into being must pass out of being," is celebrated as having reached the first stage on the path of the sage and is said to have attained the Eye of the Law—the ability to see the truth of dependent origination.

Perhaps the most sophisticated expression of the law of dependent origination is the Twelve-linked Chain of Dependent Origination, to which we turn our attention in the following chapter.

3 The Twelve-linked Chain of Dependent Origination

Throughout Buddhist history, from the days of the primitive teachings through sectarian and Mahayana Buddhism in India, China, and Japan, the Twelve-linked Chain of Dependent Origination has been the most widely employed system for explaining the Buddhist principle of causation. In the earliest sutras the number of links in the series is variously given. Sometimes the series consists of more than twelve links, in other cases of ten, nine, eight, or even two or three links. At some point the twelve-link series was established, however, and it is now the accepted interpretation. It must be remembered that the sectarian Buddhists consciously or unconsciously made alterations in the scriptures, with the result that Shakyamuni's true intent has frequently been lost. The difficulty of understanding the law of dependent origination—a difficulty on which Shakyamuni himself often commented—is aggravated by the occasional failure of the early sutras to reflect the Buddha's true meaning. Still, a return to the earliest sutras offers the best hope of formulating a logical and correct view of the chain of dependent origination, and it is on those sutras that the following discussion is based.

AN OVERVIEW

The classical statement of the Twelve-linked Chain of Dependent Origination, in the Samyutta-nikaya, is "By reason of ignorance, action; by reason of action, consciousness; by reason of consciousness, name and form; by reason of name and form, the six sense organs; by reason of the six sense organs, contact; by reason of contact, feeling; by reason of feeling, craving; by reason of craving, grasping; by reason of grasping, becoming; by reason of becoming, birth; by reason of birth, aging, death, sorrow, lamentation, misery, grief, and despair." This is the explanation of the series of conditions and causes resulting in sorrow.

The Samyutta-nikaya also explains the chain as a way of eliminating suffering: "When ignorance is eliminated, action is eliminated; when action is eliminated, consciousness is eliminated; when consciousness is eliminated, name and form are eliminated; when name and form are eliminated, the six sense organs are eliminated; when the six sense organs are eliminated, contact is eliminated; when contact is eliminated, feeling is eliminated; when feeling is eliminated, craving is eliminated; when craving is eliminated, grasping is eliminated; when grasping is eliminated, becoming is eliminated; when becoming is eliminated, birth is eliminated; when birth is eliminated, aging, death, sorrow, lamentation, misery, grief, and despair are eliminated."

The main emphasis in the Twelve-linked Chain is on the sufferings of this world and the reasons for their occurrence. Primitive sources give simple, formulaic explanations of each link without offering concrete information on the relations connecting them. This subject was left for the Abhidharma writers to elaborate upon. In spite of this lack of full explanation, Shakyamuni's most outstanding disciples seem to have understood the basic idea of dependent origination, although converts from other faiths had problems with it. For example, a well-known early sutra, the Greater Discourse on the Elimination of Craving (*Mahatanhasankhaya-sutta*), relates the story of Sati, a Buddhist monk and the son of a fisherman, who had somehow concluded that the Twelve-linked Chain deals with the transmigration of a soul or self (*atman*) of the kind posited by non-Buddhist religions. Other disciples told him he was wrong, but he remained unconvinced until, upon hearing of the matter, Shakyamuni scolded Sati and brought him around to the correct view that Buddhist causation denies the existence of a spirit or soul as an immutable entity. The very telling of this story suggests that Sati was an exception and that most of Shakyamuni's disciples understood the idea of dependent origination.

Several passages in early sutras seem to offer precedents for the concept of the chain of dependent origination. Typical of them is the following comment found in the Samyutta-nikaya on the psychological process leading to suffering and anguish: "From the eye and objects arises sight consciousness. The three fuse to create contact. From contact, feeling is generated; from feeling, craving is generated; from craving, grasping is generated; from grasping, becoming is generated; from becoming, birth is generated; from birth, aging, death, and all ensuing sufferings are generated." Beginning with the link called contact, the links cited in this passage are identical to those in the Twelve-linked Chain. The relationship among the earlier links, from the eye to craving, are explained in the famous Discourse on the Six Sixes (*Chachakka-sutta*).

The Discourse on the Six Sixes outlines six sets of six elements each to describe the evolution of mental activity. They are the six internal sense fields, the six external sense fields, the six consciousnesses, the six contacts, the six feelings, and the six cravings. The six internal sense fields refer to the five physical senses of sight, hearing, taste, smell, and touch plus mind (the mind is always included with the five senses in Buddhist thought, for a total of six, not the usual Western five). These internal sense fields are the base of all perception, physical or mental. The six external sense fields are the objects perceived by the six internal sense fields. The six consciousnesses are the awarenesses that arise as a consequence of perception at the juncture of internal and external sense fields. The six contacts are the result of the combination of internal sense fields, external sense fields, and consciousness. The six feelings refer to the arising of pain or pleasure with regard to the object perceived immediately after the emergence of consciousness. The six cravings are the reactions of like or dislike born of the feeling of pain or pleasure.

A concrete example shows how these systems interact. When the eyes view a white lily, a conscious impression is formed. Previous experience, stored in the conscious or subconscious mind, combines with the impression and results in awareness or recognition of the identity of the lily with such features as color, size, shape, and fragrance. The object, the sense impression of it, and awareness fuse to produce recognition, which causes either pleasure or pain. If the pleasure at the lily's beauty is sufficiently great, the beholder desires to possess it. If, owing to some sad association, it causes pain, the viewer may turn away from the flower.

The chart opposite will help clarify the relations among the three versions of the evolving concept of dependent origination in Buddhism. The passage examined first, from the Samyutta-nikaya, expands on the number of links set forth in the Discourse on the Six Sixes, adding the four links of grasping, becoming, birth, and aging and death. While the links beginning with contact are identical in the Samyutta-nikaya and the Twelve-linked Chain of Dependent Origination, the first three links of the Discourse on the Six Sixes (internal sense fields, external sense fields, and consciousnesses) seem at variance with the three

Discourse on the Six Sixes	Samyutta-nikaya	Twelve-linked Chain
		ignorance
		action
six internal sense fields	eye	consciousness
six external sense fields	objects	name and form
six consciousnesses	sight consciousness	six sense organs
six contacts	contact (by the fusion of the preceding three)	contact
six feelings	feeling	feeling
six cravings	craving	craving
	grasping	grasping
	becoming	becoming
	birth	birth
	aging and death	aging and death

Three versions of the concept of dependent origination

comparable links of the Twelve-linked Chain (consciousness, name and form, and the six sense organs). In fact, as will be explained in detail later, they are essentially the same in content and differ only in order of appearance in the two sources. Consciousness is the same in both systems. Name and form correspond to the external sense fields, and the six sense organs and the six internal sense fields are the same thing. In both the Discourse on the Six Sixes and the Twelve-linked Chain, these three elements or links combine to produce contact. The difference in the order in which they are arranged is insignificant, since these three links exist simultaneously and any order assigned them is merely arbitrary.

The explanation of psychological or mental evolution in the Samyutta-nikaya begins with internal sense fields, external sense fields, and consciousness. The Twelve-linked Chain, however, adds two links preceding these mental events: ignorance and action. The earliest chain of dependent origination, lacking ignorance and action, seems to have been a ten-linked one. Ignorance and action were added later, to create the present Twelve-linked Chain. Though we will discuss the reasons for this in detail below, the addition was important because ignorance and action demonstrate that our mental activities and judgments do not occur in isolation; that is, the mind is not a tabula rasa. Past mental events and experiences shape the present. Ignorance and action are crucial elements in the chain, linking it to suffering and transmigration, of which they are the sources.

THE FIRST THREE LINKS

Ignorance, the first link, means lack of knowledge of correct Buddhist principles and the truths of the world and of human existence. Failure to know the truth leads to faulty judgments and misdeeds, which bring on failure and grief. Ignorance is the fundamental cause of errors and the misfortunes they yield.

Action, the second link, is the mistaken conduct caused by ignorance. It is identical with karma. Lacking a correct view of the world and humankind, human beings think, judge, and act wrongly. Instead of ending when committed, good and bad actions persist and accumulate to reappear as causes of later actions. In other words, good and evil deeds that go undetected by others nonetheless have karmic effects on the perpetrator. In the Buddhist context, the term action means both the present deed and the accumulated deeds of the past. The sum of past deeds is of especially great importance in the Twelve-linked Chain of Dependent Origination.

Not only actions resulting from ignorance but also general experiences, whether good or bad, physical or spiritual, become a latent force constantly exerting an influence on thought and conduct. An accumulation of good deeds makes it easier to perform still more good deeds, while an accumulation of evil acts offers little to hinder the perpetration of further wickedness and aggravates the difficulty of turning in the direction of good. Each individual has a store of past actions and experiences that manifest themselves in various ways. They determine memory or intellectual capacities, temperament, skills or talents, and physique and health—in short, the total person. A person is the total of all he or she has done in the past, and action in the Twelve-linked Chain of Dependent Origination means the total of past mistaken experiences caused by ignorance within the cycle of transmigration.

In the context of the Twelve-linked Chain of Dependent Origination, consciousness signifies perception as a whole, which is based on and incorporates past experiences. Human awareness is not pure but is colored by past actions. It looks through a filter tinted by preconceptions derived from past experiences, preconceptions that make totally objective judgment and understanding impossible. Since consciousness includes elements derived from actions based on ignorance, its perceptions and their results are always mistaken.

Consciousness is both the faculty with which to perceive what is happening from moment to moment in the present and the sum total of all consciousness experienced from the past, back to the instant of birth. No two individuals, not even siblings, are born with the same intellectual abilities, personality, or physique. All are different because all have accumulated different karma. On the foundation of the unique traits present at birth, human beings proceed to perceive, judge, and act throughout life in ways influenced by the totality of past experiences. This foundation is by no means fixed and unchanging. With each new experience, the awarenesses with which the person is born are altered for better or worse. A good person may not remain good, and a bad person need not remain bad. Because the personality, or consciousness, is impermanent and without a persisting independent self, all kinds of transformations are possible, depending on the amount of effort exerted.

Because it contains all past experiences, this consciousness is comparable to what the Consciousness Only school of Buddhism called the storehouse consciousness, or *alaya-vijnana*. According to this school of thought, each good or bad experience is stored as a seed in the storehouse consciousness. The energy latent in the seeds influences future experience and evokes certain specific results. Though, as the story of the fisherman's son Sati related above suggests, non-Buddhists could try to interpret this consciousness as the permanent, immutable soul, such an interpretation is erroneous. In the Buddhist view, consciousness is constantly changing as new experiences are encountered and lacks a persisting self that might be compared to a soul. Buddhism, while recognizing karma and the personality, consistently refutes the idea of a permanently persisting self in all things.

THE REMAINING NINE LINKS

Name (mental existence) and form (material existence) include all phenomena. In the context of the Twelve-linked Chain, however, they refer specifically to mental or material phenomena as the objects of our five physical senses and the mind. The objects of the five physical senses are shapes, sounds, odors, tastes, and tactile properties—in other words, material realities. The objects of the mind are mental realities. Since name and form mean all phenomena as perceived objects, this link is equivalent to the six external sense fields of the Discourse on the Six Sixes.

The six sense organs are of course the five physical senses plus the mind. The Sanskrit term for the six sense organs is *shadayatana*, literally, "six entrances." The six sense organs were conceived of as doors through which physical and mental perception somehow enter, since the six external sense fields (name and form) enter conscious experience by means of the six sense organs.

Contact, which is the fusion of the six sense organs, six sense fields, and six consciousnesses, stimulates awareness. Implied in contact are the conditions—clarity and proximity of the object being perceived and direction of the attention toward it—that are essential if this fusion is to result in awareness. Although the formula states that contact arises from the six sense organs, this must be understood to mean that it evolves from an amalgam of the three preceding links in the chain.

Feeling means the pleasure or pain (or nonpleasure or nonpain) resulting from the recognition of an object and influenced by previous experience. Feeling is not only inherent in the object of awareness but also conditioned by past experiences. As mentioned earlier, associations may cause some people to feel sad when they see a white lily, whereas others merely take delight in the flower's beauty.

The Sanskrit word for craving, *trishna*, is sometimes translated into Chinese with a compound that means literally "desire or thirst." Craving is an instinctive impulse based on ignorance. It is as devoid of reason or logic as a thirsty person's longing for water. It is a passionate yearning for the pleasurable and rejection of the painful. Like feeling, it is influenced by past experience.

Craving is subdivided into three categories: physical craving, the craving for existence, and the craving for nonexistence. Physical craving is sensuous and includes sexual love. The craving for existence is a wish to be reborn in a paradise free of the inevitable sufferings of this world. The craving for nonexistence reflects understanding that the pleasures of a future paradise as well as those of this world are transient and that as long as existence persists human beings are fated to return to suffering. Consequently, this craving is directed toward the attainment of nothingness. Shakyamuni regarded as mistaken both his contemporaries who longed for the pleasures of this world and those who sought escape from it in annihilation, since both kinds of craving—based on ignorance—are causes of the suffering inherent in the cycle of birth, death, and rebirth. In his very first sermon, the Buddha cautioned the five ascetics who were his audience against passion as an expression of physical craving and against the craving for either rebirth in a state of bliss or total annihilation, teaching them to follow the Middle Way of liberation from ignorance.

Craving always manifests itself in the action of reaching out to acquire what is desirable or to cast away what is undesirable. This is grasping. In contrast to craving, which is an internal, mental activity, grasping is external behavior, taking what is liked and discarding what is disliked. Buddhism often divides all action—that is, karma—into mental action, physical action, and verbal action. In this case, craving is a mental action, while grasping is physical and verbal. Both, of course, are the products of ignorance and are therefore mistaken behavior.

Becoming means the potential being that accumulates as a result of craving and includes such elements of the human constitution as intellectual capacity, temperament, skills, and physique. As was pointed out in the discussion of action, becoming and all its attributes are the result of the totality of past experience.

In a broad sense, birth is the coming into being of experience influenced by the latent force of past mistakes. It is the realization of potential existence. The word birth refers to the future moments of our lives, which are governed by the total experience of our present lives. Thus birth resembles all the other links, which are mistaken because they are determined by the ignorance and erroneous action of previous existences or experiences.

Aging and death, the inevitable consequences of birth, entail with equal inevitability sorrow, lamentation, misery, grief, and despair because they reflect the mistaken thoughts and attitudes inherent in the ignorance from which birth results. Aging and death, then, are the products of the process arising from ignorance and craving.

It is important to realize that several of the links in the chain are similar in content. For instance, ignorance and craving resemble each other in that both emerge from erroneous thought and action caused by failure to view humanity and the world correctly. Action, which consists of individual examples of mistaken conduct and accumulations of such conduct, is equivalent to a combination of craving (mistaken conduct) and becoming (accumulation of wrong experience). In other words, the links called ignorance and action are essentially the same in content as the links called craving and becoming.

DUAL DEPENDENT ORIGINATION

The above explanation, the one usually found in the earliest sutras, interprets the Twelve-linked Chain of Dependent Origination psychologically, as a process beginning with ignorance and ending in suffering. Since the age of sectarian Buddhism, however, the chain has been given another interpretation, a theory of dual dependent origination spanning the past, present, and future. This interpretation attempts to explain both physical and psychological phenomena. Ignorance and action are regarded as part of the previous life, the next eight links are assigned to the present life, and the last two links are said to manifest themselves in the next life. Consciousness, the first link belonging to the present life, is the mental equipment that comes into being at the moment that a creature (human or nonhuman) is conceived. Name and form are the physical and spiritual attributes that develop in the embryo. The six sense organs are six potential sensuous powers that the embryo acquires before birth. Contact is physical birth, and feeling is the pleasure or pain the immature being experiences while being exposed to the realities of life. Craving is physical and emotional longing, such as that of young love.

twelve links	ignorance action	two past causes
	consciousness name and form six sense organs contact feeling	five present fruits
	craving grasping becoming	three present causes
	birth aging and death	two future fruits

Dual dependent origination in the three time realms

The system is referred to as dual because it includes two sets of causes and effects, one covering past and present and the other covering present and future: the first two links in the chain are past causes, of which the next five are the present fruits; craving, grasping, and becoming are present causes, and birth and aging their future fruits. Though not to be totally rejected, this interpretation is too crude to be regarded as an adequate statement of the Buddha's teaching of dependent origination.

DEPENDENT ORIGINATION AND FATE

The Twelve-linked Chain of Dependent Origination provides a concrete explanation of the way karmic relations cause the emergence of suffering from ignorance, craving, and delusion in the lives of individual human beings. In actual life, however, suffering is the result of more than an individual's karmic influences. Thoughts and actions (the three karmas of thought, word, and deed) are not the only causes and conditions that affect human beings and lead to happiness or grief. In addition to volitional karmic aspects, learning and the accumulation of knowledge and memory play a part in character formation and consequently exert strong influences on fate.

Many factors over which the individual has little or no

control also influence fate: childhood training at home or at school, social environment, natural calamities (such as flood or earthquake), human-caused disasters (such as fire or robbery), social pressures (such as those from political parties or labor unions), and so on. To these more or less identifiable forces must be added the element of apparently pure chance: missing a train that is later wrecked and thus being saved from injury or death, or rushing to board an airplane that crashes on takeoff. White-collar workers often consider good or bad luck the only possible explanation of rapid promotion or stagnation in the same job for years. Countless business deals have been concluded because someone with the right product happened to be in the right place at the right time. And a very thin line of chance is sometimes all that separates success from failure.

Some people deprecate the element of luck and argue that a person who tries can always get ahead. Successful businesspeople and politicians are especially reluctant to attribute their success to pure chance. Other people, however, see life as a game of cards in which the deck is stacked against them and are only too eager to explain their failures as the result of bad luck or the lack of good opportunities. Individual character and past experiences can alter a person's estimation of the relative importance of luck and effort in success.

Chance and inevitability are always open to question. Some people seem to be especially unlucky, to have a tiny character flaw or attitude problem that virtually invites calamity. But not everything described as inevitable is completely unrelated to human actions. For instance, damage from earthquakes or typhoons can be considerably reduced by adequate warning systems and suitable precautionary measures. By taking just such steps, many countries have greatly reduced the dangers of droughts and severe cold, calamities once ranked with typhoons and earthquakes. Obviously, human beings can take precautions to prevent such misfortunes as fire and theft, and the exercise of the public conscience could eliminate the harm done by unscrupulous political parties and labor movements. On the individual level, people are often able to turn a mishap to advantage. Others, however, are too lazy to take the opportunities for success that life presents them. In other words, diligence and cultivated capacities to a large extent determine fate.

Nevertheless, no individual human being ever has complete control over the causes of happiness or sorrow. Frequently these causes arise either partly or entirely from natural occurrences or social conditions. The philosophy of Hua-yen Buddhism makes a clear distinction between dependent origination on the purely individual level and dependent origination on the wider level, in which everything is intimately connected with everything else in both time and space. This splendid concept is illustrated in the Flower Garland Sutra, the principal scripture of the Hua-yen sect, by the image of a candle surrounded by mirrors. The light of the candle is reflected in all directions. No part of it can be described completely without describing the whole, nor can the whole be described without reference to all the parts. Nonetheless, each part has its own identifiable being.

DEPENDENT ORIGINATION AND KARMIC REWARDS

Society moves in directions that its individual members cannot easily alter. Each member is subject to the restrictions and limitations society imposes. Sometimes the individual must be sacrificed. Sometimes, while pretending to act in the general public interest, a particular class or a few powerful people profit at the expense of everyone else. Though ostensibly established to improve society, political parties and labor organizations frequently try to monopolize benefits. Nonetheless, all organizations are made up of individuals, each with an individual character and conscience that in democracies, which are supposed to be expressions of the collective will of their members, are matters of prime importance. Ultimately, the will and the deeds of the individual are considered of prime importance in Buddhism, too. This is why the Twelve-linked Chain of Dependent Origination (though it does of course include consideration of the accidental and the inevitable) concentrates on the individual's psychological activities.

Different people react differently to the same social environment. Some may find it cruel and oppressive, while others, with identical status, accept or even like it. In a given objective situation, altering the subjective approach can convert misery into joy. To a certain extent, religion teaches us to do just that, and this is why some people condemn religion as an opiate. Yet when religion can justifiably be called an opiate, the fault lies not in inherent failings of religion itself but in unscrupulous attempts by parties or groups to use the subjectivity essential to religion for self-aggrandizement. Subjectivity itself is not to blame. On the contrary, just as opium is a boon in some medical situations, so too can subjectivity in religion be most beneficial when used correctly. It has enabled religion to solve problems that resist solution by all other means. Furthermore, a subjective or spiritual approach to problems influences and thus can improve the objective aspects of life.

A person struggling with what appears to be an insuperable financial problem worries and frets, cannot sleep, and finds that food has no appeal. Failing health makes it difficult to work. The sudden advent of religious faith changes the person's attitude toward life overnight. Realizing that one can do no more than one's best, the person ceases to worry. As anxiety vanishes, the person is once again able to sleep and eat properly. Soon, healthy again, the person is able to attack work with new vigor. The person's fortunes improve, the apparently insuperable problem fades into insignificance, and before long the person is better off than ever before.

This kind of thing has happened often in the past and will continue to happen. Undeniably, a spiritual awakening can lead to improved health and even to business success. Though perhaps not its highest goal, physical and financial recovery is a frequent side effect of religious faith. Materialist critics of religion as an opiate ignore its positive effects as a subjective stimulant to objective health and prosperity. In addition, while bringing inner peace and a change of mind, religion insists that instead of resting content with an improved state of private affairs, human beings do all within their power to reform the social evils that lead to misery and strife and try to rid the world of both natural and human-caused disasters. It goes without saying that this is a prime consideration in the Buddhist law of dependent origination.

Mental aspects centered on the will and karmic influences, though not constituting the whole of human social activities, are a great moving force in them. The law of dependent origination explains all causation; the twelve links deal primarily with the roles of illusion and karma. The mental aspect, particularly the human will, is the prime cause; other factors are conditions or indirect causes.

Moreover, all actions, good and bad, are stored within human beings as latent energy influencing all subsequent conduct and attitudes. Not the slightest action is lost. Whether or not others see, whether or not the gods observe, whether or not the perpetrator is fully aware, every act remains as a phase of experience. And the accumulation of past experience shows in conduct and countenance. When continually committed, wickedness becomes a habit, evident in a gruff or insolent tone of voice, a shifty eye, a cruel look, and a scornful attitude that incurs dislike and distrust. Conversely, a person who repeatedly does and thinks good acquires a pleasant voice quality and an air of benignity that inspire admiration and affection. In other words, good or bad, ordinary habits become an unconscious part of an individual's being, apparent to all. No more eloquent testimony for the cumulative effect of experience could be furnished.

The kind of life a person has led can be discerned in every deed. The person's entire past has been absorbed into his or her character and temperament. Similarly, since causation is active in the past, present, and future, today's conduct indicates the course of tomorrow's character development. In Buddhist terms, good or bad effects of past deeds on present experience are referred to as karmic rewards; and the Twelve-linked Chain of Dependent Origination is called karma-determined dependent origination. As I have said, however, this system does not fix destiny irrevocably. A bad person need not remain bad. A good person may not remain good. The most vicious person is improved by performing a good act, and an upright person mars his or her character by committing wickedness. In other words, all acts and experiences, moment by moment, determine the individual's life.

Karma-determined dependent origination by no means explains everything people do. For instance, it fails to furnish an adequate key to psychological processes, in which good and bad seeds independent of karma are constantly at work. Mental operations are not confined to situations in which good causes good and evil causes evil. Nor are the effects of those mental operations limited to the person experiencing them. Without removing the karmic effects of past actions, a malefactor can find whole or partial salvation through repentance, for the merits that one person acquires through good deeds can be transferred (as in the case of the merits a bodhisattva transfers to others) and used to atone for others' transgressions.

Life is influenced by all kinds of natural and scientific

laws—physical, mathematical, chemical, physiological, psychological, economic, political, legal, ethical, and aesthetic. All of these standards and principles constantly intermingle and interact with one another and with karma in the complex mixture of objective and subjective phenomena that constitutes life. Under these circumstances, totally explaining dependent origination as it operates in life would involve the impossible task of mastering all fields of modern science, scholarship, and art. From the religious viewpoint, however, it is enough to try to understand how things are and to strive to determine how they should be. These are the purposes of a true understanding of dependent origination. The Twelve-linked Chain is merely a metaphoric explanation for people in early stages of development—like showing how seed, as the direct cause, in the presence of such indirect causes as warmth, moisture, air, sunlight, and fertilizers, germinates, blooms, and bears fruit.

INEXHAUSTIBLE INTERRELATIONS

Though the Twelve-linked Chain explains individual conduct in terms of karma and karmic reward, the situation is actually much more complex. Individual action is determined by an infinite variety of factors operating throughout time and space. The causal relationships of dependent origination are limitless.

A simple example related to international trade offers an idea of how this vast network of relationships functions. The Japanese people's everyday necessities are obtained through the efforts of other peoples all over the world. Nearly all woolen clothing in Japan is made of cloth woven from imported raw materials. The wheat used in bread is produced abroad, as is much of the lumber used in construction. Untold millions of workers are involved in the production, transportation, manufacture, wholesaling, and retailing of the coats the Japanese people wear. Millions more play a part in providing capital for the various industries and trades involved in the production of coal, oil, and electricity. Though some countries are less reliant on the outside world than Japan, the economic system on which modern people as a whole depend spreads over the entire globe and involves practically everybody.

Politically and socially, materially and spiritually, the whole world is interrelated. The global population has become a single society on an enormous scale. A malfunction of any part of this society affects all other parts. On the national and urban levels, everyday life is directly dependent on a wide range of intricate connections. If the water supply is cut, electric power fails, or the transportation service breaks down, all ordinary activities are soon thrown into chaos.

What is true of large and small groups is also true of the individual. The human body and mind are not separate units but interdependent parts of a whole. They thrive or languish in consonance with each other. Respiration, alimentation, circulation, metabolism, and the operations of the nervous system cooperate as parts of an integrated system. When one bodily organ fails, another may undertake its functions for a time, but eventually debility or illness sets in. The more important the organ's functions, the more serious its inability to carry them out.

All things in the great body of human society are related just as they are in the single human body. Each physical and spiritual function is dependent in some way on all others, and since present status is both the result of past causes and the cause of future results, interdependence extends through time as well as space. Limitlessly interrelated causes and effects sway the whole of history, the past, present, and future of the entire universe.

A distinction is often drawn between the inorganic on the one hand and the organic and purposeful on the other.

Though apparently mechanical, society moves in a purposeful way because all of its members are consciously goal oriented. Since they are morally neutral, the Buddhist doctrines of impermanence and the absence of a persisting self are as purposeless as the laws of physics and chemistry. The principles that all existence is suffering and that nirvana is tranquillity, however, are purposeful: their goal is the elimination of suffering, and they set standards for religious—specifically, Buddhist—ideals. A course of action is organic when it has ideal purposes, regards as evil whatever runs counter to those purposes and as good whatever conduces to their achievement, and strives to move away from evil and toward good. The Buddhist law of dependent origination regards confinement to the cycle of transmigration and suffering as evil, interprets the elimination of the causes that produce such suffering as good, and teaches the way to attain that goal.

Though most human physiological and psychological operations are carried out oblivious to ideals, a deeper inner life force, not consciously recognized, moves toward their fulfillment. Too often, however, this unconscious vitality becomes entangled with mistaken experience and thought arising from ignorance and desire. The law of dependent origination was evolved to liberate it and enable it to advance toward the attainment of true ideals.

Human purpose endows essentially morally neutral physical or chemical phenomena with qualities of good or evil. Nuclear fission and fusion, for instance, have no intrinsic moral qualities and therefore do not deserve censure in themselves. The use of these processes by human beings is evil when it results in atomic or hydrogen bombs but good when it leads to the generation of abundant energy for beneficial purposes. It is in accord with the law of dependent origination that neutral phenomena, given good conditions, produce good effects and, given bad conditions, evil effects. Eliminating each of the causes of the

Twelve-linked Chain of Dependent Origination is the way to remove bad conditions and create good ones for the sake of abiding by the highest human ideals.

Because of the limitless web of causal interrelations extending to all things, the slightest action influences everything else throughout time and space. The actions of the individual not only affect his or her own future but also influence all society for better or for worse. Since wickedness affects not only the perpetrator but the perpetrator's family and associates as well, the individual bears tremendous responsibility. An evil act disturbs the general peace and causes unhappiness. Righteous behavior, however, contributes to the happiness of all people near and far. This is the practical meaning of the theory of limitless interrelations and the Hua-yen dictum that "one is all and all is one."

According to traditional Indian theories of karma, human beings should refrain from taking life in order to escape punishment commensurate with the act. The point is less preserving the life of another creature than protecting one's own life. Still another karmic theory holds that since all beings have lived previous lives in a variety of forms before the current reincarnation, one could, in taking the life of another living creature, unwittingly harm a dead friend or relative who has returned to this world as a nonhuman being. Fundamentally shallow, this idea is held by many Buddhists who were brought up on principles of karma-determined dependent origination. It is not mistaken so much as naive.

Many Buddhist scriptures adopt a different stand and teach restraint from killing and wounding other living things out of a sympathetic and humane desire to avoid inflicting on others pain that one would not wish to undergo oneself. According to this doctrine, which resembles that of Confucian moralists, a humane course is only to be expected of human beings. The Judeo-Christian God commanded, "Thou shalt not kill," and Jesus enjoined his followers, "Love thy neighbor as thyself." Believers are expected to obey God and emulate Jesus. The question of whether Christian love applies to animals and non-Christians, however, has remained unresolved. In this instance, love is a matter of obedience, not reason. A believer whose faith is strong regards God's commandment as absolute and obeys it. One of less faith may well stray from the path. In short, the basis for Christian love is not a logical principle of universal applicability but a creed accepted on faith.

The fundamental Buddhist viewpoint, based on the law of dependent origination, is that society is an organic macrocosm composed of interrelated individuals, all sharing responsibility for the common welfare. To kill or injure others is to obstruct the general peace and happiness. Selfishness, which disregards the needs of the the rest of the world, contradicts this principle of universal interdependence. No one can be completely happy unless the society in which he or she lives is happy and prosperous. True peace can become a reality only in a world where people neither sin nor are sinned against. Egotism and class struggle directed at the advancement of personal or group interests without regard for the welfare of others offer no hope of ultimate happiness. The way to achieve personal happiness while helping society move in the right direction is to forget oneself and consider the good of the entire social body, always recognizing the rights of one's fellows and maintaining a lofty, objective general outlook. Although this ideal stance is not easy to adopt or uphold, bearing it constantly in mind and moving steadily forward are of the greatest importance. This is the way of true democracy, a system that finds its optimum expression and its foundation in the law of dependent origination and the limitless interrelation of all beings everywhere.

4 The Pathway to Faith

The three (or four) seals of the Law, the law of dependent origination, and the Four Noble Truths express basic Buddhist views, all of which are closely related. From the theoretical viewpoint, the law of dependent origination, which describes life and society as they actually exist, is central. The focal point of religious practice, on the other hand, is the Four Noble Truths, which embody not only the logical truth of dependent origination but also moral values and the path of action whereby the Buddhist ideal can be attained.

The insight gained through an understanding of the law of dependent origination makes it possible to see the true condition of the world. Once the vast gap separating the actual world and humanity from the ideal is realized, the individual begins to yearn to abandon the flawed and sullied and to seek perfection. Realistic observation of life inspires the pursuit of the ideal once a person has come to see that actuality and the ideal, though apparently different, are not two totally separate things after all. To inspire this realization is the function of faith.

In Buddhism, the relation between theory and practice is extremely close. Theory is the foundation of practice, and practice is invariably backed by rational theory. This is as it should be. Religious practice without a sound rational basis tends to degenerate into superstition and error, and even the most splendid theory is empty if it cannot become the basis of action and find application in faith. Since the time of Shakyamuni, all Buddhist teachings, Hinayana and Mahayana alike, have held that the unity of theory and practice is essential to the creation of an ideal religion.

The doctrines of universal impermanence and the absence of a persisting self are based on an objective view of reality but motivate religious practice. These doctrines mean that all things are constantly changing, that nothing is a fixed entity, and that all existence is relative and interdependent. Realization of these truths helps prevent attachments to the transient phenomena of the world and inspires the wish to avoid harming others and to make each passing moment as valuable as possible for everyone. People who understand impermanence and the absence of a persisting self are unlikely to fritter away their short lives in vain pursuits. Aware of the pricelessness of their material and spiritual heritage, which has been created through the labor, talent, and devotion of countless people, they feel obliged to do what they can to preserve it for future generations. Such people know that precisely because it is impermanent life must not be lived carelessly.

In Buddhism religious faith and practice are based on the Four Noble Truths and the Eightfold Path, which are eloquently explained in primitive Buddhist scriptures. The prime requisite for all Buddhists, however, is faith in the Three Treasures—the Buddha, the Law, and the Order—which subsume both theory and practice. This has been recognized since ancient times, in every country to which Buddhism has spread, including Japan.

Prince Shotoku (574–622), one of the most important early Japanese patrons of Buddhism, is credited with having written a "seventeen-article constitution" for the guidance of the nation. The second article reads, in part: "Sincerely revere the Three Treasures, which are the Buddha, the Law, and the Order, for they are the final refuge of monks and nuns and male and female lay believers and the ultimate objects of worship in all countries. What person in what generation can fail to hold this Law in reverence?" In the third century B.C., the Indian emperor Ashoka urged not only his own subjects but also the peoples of all the foreign lands with which he had contact to follow the Buddhist Law, no matter what their beliefs had been before. Emphasis on the central importance of the Law was the means both the Indian emperor and the Japanese prince used to convey Buddhism to large numbers of people. It is interesting to examine the approach that Shakyamuni himself took toward people who, like many today, knew nothing of the Law, did not believe in Buddhism, and did not revere the Three Treasures.

THE GATEWAY TO FAITH

When Prince Shotoku wrote that the Three Treasures are "the ultimate objects of worship in all countries," he was expressing a wish, not a fact. Then, as in Shakyamuni's own time, many people did not hold the Three Treasures in reverence. In all ages, there are large numbers of people who feel no need of religion at all.

Buddhist sources say that in Shakyamuni's day there were sixty-two "mistaken philosophies" in India. That precise number is, of course, the contribution of later Buddhist scholars, but Shakyamuni himself denounced several widely held theories contemporary with his own philosophy. In his sermons, he made it clear that to lead people to Buddhism it is first necessary to show them the fallacies of other religions and philosophies and motivate them to abandon the mistaken practices encouraged by such systems.

More than one of the philosophies attacked by the Buddha were based on the idea that present reality constitutes nirvana, or the ideal existence. According to this view, the only way to deal with life is to accept it and try to enjoy it. In short, human beings should try to find the greatest possible pleasure in the present moment and forget about both past and future: for the hedonist, religious faith becomes superfluous. But history shows beyond doubt that such philosophies lead to the kind of decadence that has undermined many empires and civilizations. In that it does seek an ideal and is therefore not utterly without values, this philosophy may be better than none at all. Nonetheless, the dominance of pleasure seeking, an unwholesome trend today in young and old alike, is disturbing.

The condition of people who are guided by instinct or impulse alone might be called prehedonistic. In it there is no ideal, no appreciation of pleasure or pain, and no thought beyond instinct. Though religious people should be concerned with their welfare, people acting solely on the stimuli of instinct and impulse and lacking the ability to reason are beyond the range of religion's appeal. To seek religion, a person must at least be able to contemplate pleasure or pain and must be sufficiently intelligent to have ideals, even if they are no loftier than the desire to avoid pain and experience pleasure. Obviously, intelligence and ideals are no guarantee against hedonism; and without guidance, they do not always prevail against flawed philosophies. Even a serious seeker of truth may mistake a false ideal for a real one or hit upon a real one but choose the wrong way of achieving it.

As a preliminary step for the uninformed or misinformed, the pleasure seeker as well as the misguided ascetic, the Buddha taught the triple doctrine: (1) if one gives to the poor and (2) observes the five precepts, (3) one can expect to be reborn in paradise. Shakyamuni not only advocated this karmic doctrine—based on the most widely current idea of cause and effect of the time—but also considered understanding of the principle of causation on which it rests to be a prerequisite for admission to his group of followers. The triple doctrine is a classic example of the way in which Buddhist theory and practice overlap. The first two doctrines, giving and abiding by the precepts, are exhortations. The third is a promise of reward. The Buddha was saying that to become one of his followers, the Indians of his day had only to accept the doctrine that good causes produce good effects and bad causes produce bad effects.

The idea of karma had been common in India for at least two hundred years before Shakyamuni was born. The Buddha was employing this well-known principle to teach people that anyone who gave food, clothing, or shelter to the poor or to people of religion or who abided by the five precepts (not to take life, not to steal, not to indulge in wrong sexual activity, not to lie, and not to drink intoxicants) would, because good causes produce good effects, be reborn in paradise. Of course, because bad causes produce bad effects, any person who hoarded wealth and violated the precepts would be reborn in hell, the realm of hungry spirits, or the world of animals.

Those who could not learn this simple lesson in karma could not hope to comprehend the law of dependent origination or the Four Noble Truths. Comprehension of the triple doctrine enabled aspirants to cleanse their minds of false doctrines and preconceptions. Once the dross had been purged away, they were ready to move on to more advanced teachings. In other words, the Buddha employed a method of gradual guidance leading from the easy to the hard. Several primitive sutras contain passages like the following, explaining this gradual approach:

"To one seated before him, the World-honored One preached the Law gradually. First he taught giving, obeying the precepts, and [thereby] rising to heaven. Then he explained that selfish desires are evil and the cause of both misfortune and impurity, whereas separating oneself from selfish desires is a great virtue. This teaching made the heart of the listener malleable and receptive; the person put aside prejudices and experienced the ecstasy of faith. When this happened, the World-honored One for the first time preached the Four Truths of suffering, desire, nirvana, and the Way. As freshly washed and bleached fabric receives the dye, the listener received the Four Truths. While still seated there, the listener acquired the pure and unsullied Eye of the Law [which sees that all things arising from causes are ultimately extinguished]."

Not all of Shakyamuni's contemporaries accepted the idea of cause and effect. Some rejected it flatly; others accepted it but misinterpreted the relation between cause and effect. The misinterpretations of the relation between cause and effect are classified in Buddhist literature as those denying cause and effect, those admitting cause but denying effect, and those denying cause but admitting effect. One thinker espousing the first category was Purana-Kassapa, who insisted that no amount of good and no amount of wickedness have any effect on the fate of the perpetrator. Philosophers like Purana-Kassapa deal in abstract metaphysical hypotheses—that ultimate existence is eternal and immutable, is subject to neither birth nor death, and has no cause and no effect. In Buddhist terminology, this idea is rejected as eternalism, the most telling flaw of which is that even if there is an eternal existence, it cannot be known to human beings and consequently has no bearing on life. Other views belonging in the same category are those that deny the existence of good and evil; those that deny the existence of the past, present, and future; and those that deny all causation, including karma.

The second classification is something of an anomaly, since by definition causes cannot exist without effects. What is meant by this classification, however, is the severance of continuity between cause and effect. The nihilistic belief that neither spirit nor life persists after death is a philosophy admitting cause and denying effect. Buddhism rejects this approach too as annihilationism, the opposite of eternalism. The fatalism of Makkhali-Gosala, who believed that human life is totally predetermined, falls into this category, since, while admitting that human beings can act in good or bad ways, it rejects the idea that good and evil produce effects. Other similar philosophies are belief in immutable divine will or in destiny completely controlled by acts in previous existences. Buddhism considers both eternalism and annihilationism extremes to be avoided.

The third category, in which cause is rejected and effect admitted, includes philosophies asserting that everything comes into being and happens by sheer accident. The teachings of Ajita-Kesakambali and others of the six heterodox philosophers fall into this category. Since causality was a central theme in his teachings, Shakyamuni naturally considered all theories that rejected it erroneous and pernicious. While often leading ostensibly harmless lives as ascetics, proponents of such ideas were inevitably forced by their own reasoning to deny both morality and freedom of will.

MISTAKEN THEORIES OF CAUSATION

Certain religions and philosophies current in the Buddha's time recognized causality but drew incorrect connections between cause and effect. In other words, they were unable to demonstrate the relationship between assumed cause and assumed effect. Later Buddhist thinkers divided these systems into those involving false causes and those involving mistaken practices.

In the first category, a cause is invented though none is demonstrable. For instance, the idea that both the world of reality and human fate are determined by such gods as

Brahma or Indra is false because no causal relation can be shown to exist between such deities and what people do or become. Into the same category falls fatalism, the notion that destiny is determined irrevocably by the way the elements of earth, water, fire, and air combine at the instant of one's birth or by the social class into which one is born.

In the second category, practices that cannot possibly serve as causes of desired effects are performed in the hope of their efficacy. This category includes a number of superstitions current in the Buddha's time, such as the idea that imitating the actions of certain animals, covering the body with dirt and ashes, or bathing in a sacred river would lead to rebirth in paradise. The belief that certain days, compass directions, or astrological phenomena are conducive to good or bad luck falls into the same category. (Even today, the Indian people are burdened with similar forms of superstition that the Buddha preached against. In supposedly enlightened Japan, too, people avoid the numbers nine and four because they are pronounced like other words meaning suffering and death, respectively. It is customary to omit both nine and four in numbering hospital and hotel rooms.)

Other contemporary notions that were rejected for want of correct demonstrable causal links included the beliefs that meditation alone leads to nirvana or can cause the meditator to be reborn in paradise and the fanatic idea that fasting and asceticism, which are thought to free the mind, will lead to perfect freedom if practiced to the point of death.

Before achieving enlightenment, Shakyamuni studied meditation under the hermit-sages Alara-Kalama and Uddaka-Ramaputta. Although he soon learned to reach the mystic state of nothingness and then the supreme *dhyana* (meditation) in which neither perception nor nonperception exists, he was dissatisfied with his experience because he realized that meditation cannot carry one beyond life and death to nirvana, or complete tranquillity. Abandoning meditation, he spent six years practicing various forms of extreme asceticism, only to conclude ultimately that they too fail to lead to nirvana. Both meditation and asceticism rest on the assumption that mind and body are separate, when they are in fact so closely related as to be inseparable. Whatever state of mental freedom meditation is capable of producing lasts only as long as the meditation itself. Once returned to normal life, the meditator is again subject to the bonds imposed by the body and its environment. In other words, the freedom of meditation is temporary.

The idea that meditation or self-destruction through asceticism frees a spirit after the death of the body posits the existence somewhere of a spirit world. Once again, the general Buddhist view is that even if it exists, such a spirit world has no relation to the ordinary world of human experience. The goal of Buddhism is not the attainment of a fictitious paradise but the conversion of the actual world into an ideal realm—a Buddha Land. In practice, believers in meditation and asceticism as ways to nirvana are usually seeking personal escape from this life. They may achieve their end, but true happiness is not to be gained by self-centered means. It can be realized only when all human-kind has reached a state of peace and happiness.

The Buddhist law of dependent origination teaches that everything in the universe is interrelated and that all human beings live in an organically structured world, all of whose parts are interdependent. To attempt to divorce oneself from the whole and seek no more than one's own personal bliss is to ignore the principle of universal causa-tion and the moral code it implies. This is why the Buddha rejected both meditation and asceticism as paths to en-lightenment: both mistake a false cause for a true one.

5 The Religious Spirit

AWAKENING

People whose lives are guided only by instinct or impulse and who lack the mental capacity to contemplate pain and pleasure are on the lowest level with respect to religious feelings and ideals. One stage higher, but still at a prereligious level, are the fairly numerous human beings who accept reality as it is and know no greater ideal than that of satisfying their desire for pleasure and comfort. People at these two levels feel no basic dissatisfaction with the state of the world and have no urge to try to improve it. If their creature instincts are fulfilled, they are satisfied.

If the world were truly an ideal place to live in, joyful and happy, it would be difficult to disapprove of this attitude. Only to the extent that one envisions a higher way of life does the discrepancy between the real world and the ideal become obvious. There is no need for religion in the Utopian realm called Uttara-kuru, which, according to ancient Buddhist cosmology, lies north of Mount Sumeru (the center of the universe), and where all wishes come true. The Buddha never appeared in Uttara-kuru because the people dwelling there felt no need of the salvation he offered. But in the ever-changing world of reality, people are never completely satisfied, few are happy all of the time, and many are often miserable. The higher a person's ideals, the more painfully he or she realizes how far the world is from perfection. Serious consideration of the human condition generates dissatisfaction with reality; and when science, economics, and other secular disciplines and systems prove unable to eliminate this malaise, people turn to religious faith.

The large number of people in ancient India who abandoned secular life for the pursuit of religious truth illustrates the desire to dispel dissatisfaction with reality. Though blessed with riches and a happy home, Shakyamuni himself was driven by discontent with the world to leave his family and seek lofty ideals. Intolerable dissatisfaction with reality generates a deep yearning for religion and its higher truths. Only people who experience this longing can be said to have a powerfully religious spirit.

Most people, however, fail to recognize their own need for faith and have no clear concept of the ideal life, which they are therefore in no position to seek. To overcome the ignorance and relieve the suffering of such people, Shakyamuni explained the ideal of human life and the way to awaken the religious spirit (or concern with religious matters). To this end he taught the triple doctrine, in which he not only delineated good and evil but also explained karmic causal relations and offered a vision of paradise to sensitize the consciences of his listeners and give them a lofty goal. As the passage on gradual guidance quoted in the preceding chapter shows, the Buddha followed this teaching with the explanation that instinctive selfish desires are the cause of suffering and that it is necessary to divorce oneself from such desires in order to lead an ideal life.

Shakyamuni realized that people tend to have a distorted view of life, to fear what is not fearsome and to be indifferent to what is. They interpret impurity as purity, sorrow as joy, impermanence as permanence, and uncertainty as stability. The first step in teaching them what is right is to show them what is wrong.

According to a well-known story, before embarking on his search for enlightenment Shakyamuni journeyed forth from the palace in Kapilavastu, on four occasions. He encountered a sick man, an old man, a corpse, and a sage. These encounters made him aware of the suffering of illness, aging, and death and kindled in him a desire to find a universal remedy for such suffering. Though perhaps apocryphal, this account suggests that awareness of the realities of life inspired Shakyamuni to seek a higher truth.

In the Dhaniya-sutta, a dialogue between the rich cattle herder Dhaniya and Shakyamuni Buddha that is one of the oldest of all Buddhist texts, Dhaniya exults over his fortunate status. He has a beautiful and faithful wife, his children are healthy, he lives in a fine house on the bank of the Mahi River, he has many head of cattle, and he supports himself with his own earnings. Secure and comfortable, he is able to challenge the elements: "Rain, O sky, if you like!" To each of Dhaniya's statements, the Buddha replies with a comment on his own status. His house is roofless, he abides but one night on the banks of the Mahi before moving on to an uncertain destination, and his life is full of change and impermanence. Nonetheless, because the Buddha has conquered passion, wickedness, and desire, he too can say, "Rain, O sky, if you like!" Though it may seem cruel, the Buddha shattered Dhaniya's complacency to teach him the fragility of worldly happiness and open his eyes to a higher realm of existence. Moved by the Buddha's words, Dhaniya and his wife abandoned the secular life to devote themselves to the Buddha's teachings.

DEVELOPMENT

Fear of and revulsion against reality give rise to the religious spirit. Called *samvega* in Sanskrit, it results from a combined awareness of impermanence, suffering, and the absence of a persisting self and consciousness of what is holy (the ideal). Japanese believers in the teachings of the True Pure Land (Jodo Shin) sect refer to this emotion as awareness of evil, vanity, and helplessness. Christians call it a sense of guilt. All of these terms point to a fundamental discovery that the world is not what it ought to be and that life is ordinarily lived in vain. Only when a person experiences such a sense of futility and loathing are his or her eyes opened to the existence of a higher ideal, attainable by overcoming baser human instincts. Only then can such a person begin to seek the truth. The awakening of the religious spirit—sometimes called conversion—entails an about-face in one's way of thinking and living.

The true spirit of religion does not arise from a desire for economic security or a hope of being cured of disease. Worship inspired by the prospect of worldly benefits is not true worship and does not accord with the higher teachings of the Buddha. It cannot be denied, however, that many people whose original motive for turning to religion was desire for mundane well-being have gone on to acquire consciousness of higher ideals and awareness of the genuine meaning of faith. The religious experience can occur on many levels. The acquisition of the religious spirit is more often than not gradual, and ideals tend to become loftier and deeper as experience grows.

To burn with fervor is not always to be aware of religion's highest purposes. A spirit of religion resulting from a dislike of the realities of life need not be of the loftiest and purest kind. The ideals on which it is based may be inadequate, or the means employed in their attainment may be imperfect. The Indian holy men whom the Buddha criticized all sought religious ideals of one kind or another. But from the Buddha's viewpoint their ideals were false and their religious practices were therefore incorrect. Even for the Buddha himself, conversion was not final enlightenment. After becoming aware of the vanity of human life and setting forth in search of the truth, he spent seven years studying and practicing various kinds of self-discipline before discovering the true ideal and the means of achieving it.

The religion with the highest ideals and the most logical means of achieving them is the best religion. Shakyamuni presented the high ideals of Buddhism to his audiences in a logical, gradual method, suiting his message to the wisdom and capacity of each individual, as illustrated by the story of the Buddha's half brother Nanda. When Shakyamuni left home for the religious life, the Shakyas were without a crown prince and Nanda, upon reaching the age of twenty, was named to succeed Shakyamuni. At his coronation Nanda was to marry Sundari, the most beautiful woman in the kingdom. As the time of the ceremony approached, it happened that the Buddha paid his first visit to Kapilavastu since his enlightenment, and he set about converting the Shakyas to the new faith he had founded. Just before the wedding, the Buddha called at the palace to beg food and gave his empty alms bowl to Nanda, who took it to the kitchen, filled it, and started to return to the gate. Sundari saw him and asked him to come to her at once. Nanda replied that there was no need to worry. He would return before her makeup dried. When he reached the gate, however, the Buddha was gone. Nanda sought him and finally found him in Nigrodha Garden. Accepting the bowl of food, the Buddha took the opportunity to persuade Nanda to take the tonsure and become a monk.

After joining the Order, however, Nanda could not keep his mind off Sundari and the crown he had given up. Unable to carry out his religious duties properly, he complained to his fellow monks that he would like to become a layman again. Soon word of Nanda's pining for Sundari reached the ears of the Buddha, who summoned the young man for a talk. Having heard Nanda's explanation, he used his supernatural powers to transport the two of them to the realm of the thirty-three gods, where they found five hundred heavenly nymphs of unbelievable beauty playing and amusing themselves. The Buddha asked Nanda who was more beautiful, Sundari or the nymphs. The young man replied that Sundari could not compare with the heavenly beauties. The difference was as great, he said, as that between Sundari herself and an ugly old female monkey. The Buddha then promised Nanda that if he would remain a monk and live a pure life, following the discipline faithfully, after death he would be reborn in the realm of the thirty-three gods to live with the beautiful nymphs. Enticed by this prospect, Nanda forgot about Sundari and began performing his religious duties assiduously.

Because they knew he was being good for the wrong reason, his fellow monks laughed at him. They scorned one who followed the discipline out of nothing more than the hope of being rewarded with a bevy of beautiful women. But, still determined to purify Nanda's mind, the Buddha took the young man on another supernatural journey—this time to one of the most terrifying sectors of hell. Surprised to find no sinners being tortured there, Nanda asked why and was told that this particular place in hell had been prepared for a disciple named Nanda, who was performing religious duties for evil purposes and would eventually be taken there for punishment. This frightened Nanda so greatly that he changed his way of thinking entirely and became a truly righteous follower of the Buddha.

The lives of great Buddhist priests contain many stories of men who became monks to acquire fame or position and later, through study and practice, became genuine believers. Though the story of Nanda is a fabrication of a later date, it may well be true that the Buddha's half brother advanced from a lower to a higher level of faith as a result of the Buddha's intervention. Concern for religion may start with various motives. It may be less a dissatisfaction with reality than a desire for status or profit. It may begin as indefinite theoretical or philosophical curiosity or as mere habit. Furthermore, the fear of reality that leads some people to religion varies in degree and intensity and therefore may be expected to result in equally varied degrees of faith. But it is the religious spirit, no matter what its source, that is the fundamental force inspiring people to seek the ideal state.

In the initial stage, dissatisfaction with the actual world is usually a private matter. Typically, a person longs to escape from the world of suffering and transmigration to eternal nirvana. But this yearning remains concerned with karmic rewards and with the individual's own pain and pleasure. People who understand the true principle of dependent origination and discover the highest aim of Buddhism realize that they cannot find happiness through their own salvation alone and that the true aim of human life must be the achievement of peace and well-being for society as a whole. Having reached this point, such people reject the self-oriented for the world-oriented vision. Instead of worrying about their own comfort and peace of mind, they become altruistic enough to fall into lower states of being (the realms of hell, hungry spirits, and beasts) for the sake of saving others. Less noble motives recede into the background or are rejected altogether. This step-by-step advancement accounts for the complexity of religious phenomena and for the expedient methods of Buddhist guidance, in which each teaching is adjusted to the need of the moment, just as medication must be selected to suit the illness being treated.

THE FOUR INDESTRUCTIBLE OBJECTS OF FAITH

The ultimate ideal of Buddhism is to purify all society in accord with the principles of dependent origination and the

Four Noble Truths. Eventually the process must transcend the confines of karmic-reward theories. As noted in the discussion of gradual teaching, the karma-oriented triple doctrine is followed by the teaching of the law of dependent origination in the form of the Four Noble Truths. The person who has mastered these is said to have acquired the pure Eye of the Law, or the wisdom required to form right views of the world and humanity. Such a person's understanding of Buddhism is so firm that he or she is no longer in danger of being lured away by false creeds or philosophies and of thus being prevented from attaining enlightenment. After the primitive period, Buddhism referred to this state, in which faith is fixed and definite, as the stage of beholding the truth of no reincarnation or the true nature in which there is no more birth, and regarded it as the lowest of the stages leading to enlightenment.

This state can be attained in two ways: intellectually or by pure faith. Unenlightened people can find enlightenment in the teachings of others or in study. Holders of wrong views can be taught how to correct them by gradual instruction. Depending on the individual's nature and way of thinking, however, it is possible to attain the same state through faith without intellectual guidance. People fond of theorizing are usually receptive to the intellectual method of gradual instruction. Those who are more emotionally oriented may be guided by faith alone. For the ordinary person, faith is the less demanding method in terms of time and training.

Yet practice in accordance with faith has the advantage of appealing to people who, lacking pronounced religious urges, follow Buddhism through habit. Recent surveys show that although many people are converted to faith as a result of fear of sickness or death or because of a general dread of reality, many others embrace religious faith only to follow in their parents' footsteps. In the Buddha's day, too, there were people who accepted faith out of custom or family tradition. As they devoted themselves to the Three Treasures and grew to the condition in which their faith was fixed and definite, however, they came to believe absolutely in what are called the four indestructible objects of faith: the Buddha, the Law, the Order, and the precepts. The early scriptures contain numerous formulaic mentions of these four. One of the most notable is found in the famous Pali Sutra of the Great Decease (*Mahaparinibbana-sutta*).

Having left the kingdom of Magadha and crossed the Ganges to Vajji, the Buddha took lodging in the village of Nadika, where his disciple Ananda, speaking for a great company of followers, asked what had happened to a number of lay believers who had already died. Instead of relating the fate of each person individually, the Buddha replied, "Now there is nothing strange in this, Ananda, that a human being should die; but that as each one does so you should come to me and inquire about them is wearisome for me. I will, therefore, teach you a way of truth, called the Mirror of the Law, which if a disciple of the noble one possess he may, if he should so desire, himself predict of himself: 'I will neither go to hell, nor be reborn as a beast, nor go to the realm of the hungry spirits. I have left the world of suffering and entered into the stream of sanctification [the lowest level on the path of the sage]. I am assured of hereafter attaining the enlightenment of the *arhat*.'

"What then, Ananda, is this Mirror of the Law? It is the consciousness that the disciple is possessed of faith in the Buddha—believing the Exalted One to be Worthy of Respect, Omniscient, Perfect in Knowledge and Conduct, Well-gone, Understander of the World, Unsurpassed, Controller, Teacher of Gods and Men, the Buddha, and the World-honored One. And that he [the disciple] is possessed of faith in the Law—believing the Law to have been proclaimed by the Exalted One, of advantage in this world, passing not away, welcoming all, leading to salvation, and to be attained by the wise, each one for himself. And then he [the disciple] is possessed of faith in the Order—believing the multitude of the disciples of the Exalted One who are walking in the eight stages of effort and attainment, the righteous, the upright, the just, the law-abiding—believing this Order of the Exalted One to be worthy of honor, of hospitality, of gifts, and of reverence; to be the supreme sowing ground of merit for the world; to be possessed of the virtues beloved by the good, virtues unbroken, intact, unspotted, unblemished, virtues that make men truly free, virtues that are praised by the wise, are untarnished by the desire of future life or by belief in the efficacy of outward acts, and are conducive to concentration of the heart."

Though this passage, like many others in the sutras, is somewhat difficult to follow, its general meaning is that the Mirror of the Law reflects the truth—revealing the fates of believers after death—and is identical with the four indestructible objects of faith. The Mirror reveals the person who has complete faith in the Three Treasures and abides strictly by the discipline to be progressing steadfastly toward enlightenment and no longer subject to rebirth in the world of suffering.

Even if Buddhist doctrines are not fully understood, a person can escape the perplexity caused by other teachings and proceed steadily, in accordance with the Law, toward enlightenment if he or she believes that the Buddha was a perfect human being worthy of the ten honorific epithets enumerated in the passage quoted above; that the Law he preached is absolute truth, the supreme medicine for curing the evils that attack people's spirits; and that the Order is composed of trustworthy, respectable monks who deserve to be regarded as leaders. Since his or her daily life will be in complete accord with the precepts, such a person will escape the suffering caused by moral transgression. Obedience to the precepts will be so natural that he or she will require no coercion to stay on the correct path. Such a person will be able to stand alone, confidently leading a good life and indifferent to whether others observe his or her actions.

A person who is devoted to the four indestructible objects of faith feels no urge to cheat in small ways because "no one will know" or because "everyone else is doing it." The world would be a far better place if all people had the kind of faith that prevents them from committing even minor transgressions.

THE TRIPLE DOCTRINE AND THE
FOUR INDESTRUCTIBLE OBJECTS OF FAITH

Karmic reward, the foundation of the triple doctrine, is acceptable only on an elementary level, where it serves as an introduction to more profound tenets of Buddhist philosophy, such as the Four Noble Truths and the law of dependent origination.

The doctrine of the four indestructible objects of faith, though requiring no theoretical understanding and therefore different in approach, is nonetheless based on observance of Buddhist ideals and is related to the triple doctrine. For example, the precepts as an indestructible object of faith include both giving and the precepts themselves, and are thus equivalent to the first two of the three doctrines. The triple doctrine, however, leads only to birth in heaven, which is, as we have seen, impermanent, while the teaching of the four indestructible objects of faith leads eventually to nirvana. In short, although the triple doctrine is limited to the realm of karma, the teaching of the four objects of faith transcends karma. On the preliminary level of the triple doctrine, a person does good because of the promise of karmic reward. There is nothing wrong with this. But it is incomparably more worthy to do good for its own sake.

This point is illustrated by a famous story about the sixth-century Indian priest Bodhidharma, who is said to have founded Ch'an (Zen, in Japanese) Buddhism in China, and the emperor Wu Ti of the Liang dynasty (r. 502–45). The emperor is reported to have asked Bodhidharma, "Since I became ruler, I have built many temples and monasteries, permitted many men to become monks, held countless Buddhist services and ceremonies, and done everything I could to promote Buddhism. What merits have these good deeds gained me?" Bodhidharma replied simply to the emperor, who was obviously proud of his record, "No merits at all."

Failing to understand the true meaning of Buddhism, the emperor assumed that his support of the faith would ensure that his empire would flourish and his descendants would rule through eternity. It did not occur to him that he should have done good to make his people happy, as the Indian emperor Ashoka did before him and the Japanese prince Shotoku did after him. Bodhidharma hoped to shock the emperor into a realization of the true intent of Buddhism.

Buddhist teachings urge charity because bestowing material goods and the Law on others is the best way to promote psychological harmony in the recipients and contribute to social welfare. This works even in small ways. Sharing something with others inspires friendship, even if the givers grudge the reduction of their own wealth and are truly concerned with only their own security and happiness. Someone who, after hearing the teaching of giving and its karmic rewards, makes a gift to a person in need—even if grudgingly—is greeted with a gratitude more enthusiastic than he or she has ever encountered. Thus the giver sees that giving not only delights the receiver but also warms the heart of the giver. Perhaps shut up within themselves before, givers break down the wall between themselves and others as a result of acts of charity. Givers and recipients surmount the barriers between them and experience the warmth of encounters that lead to amity and harmony.

At the outset, a person may engage in charitable works in the hope of the karmic reward of rebirth in paradise. But as the experience is repeated the person forgets about rewards and gives for the pleasure of giving, eventually advancing to the realization that even this pleasure is selfish. Warmed by the light and peace generated by giving, such a person finds life meaningless without giving selflessly and no longer even takes into consideration the pleasure to be derived from acts of giving.

A doctrine called the threefold circle of purity explains true altruism as that in which no reckoning is made of the giver, the recipient, or the gift. In other words, the giver is unconscious of self and act, the recipient, and the value of the gift, and gives no thought to the recompense or the honor such acts might earn. This is similar to the way in which a person who is truly devoted to keeping the precepts needs no instructions, threats, or rewards but abides by the rules to avoid strife and unhappiness. A child of three can be made to understand that doing evil is wrong and doing good is right. But many people of three score or more cannot put the principle into practice.

The person who is devoted to the four indestructible objects of faith does good as a matter of course. The admonition of the seven buddhas "to do no evil, to do all good, to purify one's mind" underscores the need to have faith so powerful and pure that evil is impossible. Dogen had this in mind when he said, "The power of self-discipline is manifest when one is no longer capable of doing any evil at all." There are various paths whereby this condition of unshakable purity can be reached: belief in the four indestructible objects of faith, Zen meditation, chanting the name of Amitabha Buddha, and so on. All these ways lead to the state in which morality and discipline are no longer needed, since wrongdoing is impossible.

This is the correct course of development of Buddhist faith and practice. Through the Buddha's method of gradual guidance, believers receive the Eye of the Law, which enables them to understand the Four Noble Truths and the law of dependent origination. Devotion to the four indestructible objects of faith protects them from false philosophies. Their concept of humankind and the universe is correct in a way only Buddhism makes possible. Their faith in the Three Treasures is firm, and they are no longer capable of violating the precepts. From this condition they advance to the stage at which they no longer need to think about suffering or nirvana. Assured of buddhahood, they are able to reside in the actual world of cause-and-effect relations without becoming attached to or being swayed by its phenomena. They have transcended cause and effect. Instead of fearing or shunning existence in the world of transience, they welcome it and work to convert that world into the ideal realm, known in Buddhism as the Pure Land.

6 The Four Noble Truths

The major purpose of all religions is to cure the illnesses of the spirit and create a wholesome, integrated psychological condition. Most religions therefore include methods for dealing with partial and temporary mental disturbances, which can be compared with such physical ailments as toothaches, boils, or diarrhea. In the most primitive religions, magical practices and incantations are intended to deal with just such disturbances. Some of Japan's new religious organizations specialize in ways of bringing about temporary solutions to human problems; the higher religions also include methods devoted to similar aims. But religion's major task is the essential improvement of the psychological being to ensure spiritual health and immunity to spiritual illness.

Most people who show no symptoms of pathological conditions (everyone has the odd minor complaint, of course) consider themselves in good physical shape. But meticulous examination of the organs and systems of the body usually reveals defects of one kind or another. In other words, from the medical standpoint few people are completely healthy. Even people with nothing specifically wrong with them generally have physical weak points. Furthermore, it is always desirable to maintain and improve one's good health.

In similar fashion, most people who feel no particular spiritual suffering assume they are in a sound state of psychological health. Many remain unaware of their true condition because they do not recognize the difference between spiritual health and spiritual illness. Without a reliable criterion, they consider the unhealthy to be sound and believe themselves free of mental suffering and in no need of help from religion. Even those who are relatively sound of spirit, like those in good physical shape, need to maintain and improve their health. They need to deepen their religious faith and discipline and cultivate themselves in order to preserve and improve the psychological health they enjoy. The teachings of the Four Noble Truths and the Eightfold Path are the foundation of a highly rational system that not only corrects spiritual disturbances but also promotes overall spiritual health and encourages its improvement.

Like a great physician of the mind, Shakyamuni taught the four truths that life is suffering, that ignorance is the cause of suffering, that suffering can be eliminated, and that the Eightfold Path is the way to eliminate suffering. A medical doctor must accurately diagnose the cause of a patient's illness and must know the nature of the illness when it is recognized. Shakyamuni taught that we must accurately understand the nature of human suffering. This is the significance of the first of the four truths.

After determining the nature of the illness from which a patient is suffering, the doctor must correctly diagnose the cause of the pathological state. The Buddha understood the need to find the cause of suffering, that is, the nature of the obstacle to perfect human spiritual health. Just as it is impossible to ensure adequate treatment for a disease whose causes are imperfectly understood, so it is impossible to eliminate suffering unless its cause is clearly understood. Inevitably, suffering and its stimulus are bound together by causal links, and suffering will not vanish as long as the stimulus persists. The second of the four truths sets forth the cause of suffering.

To effect a cure, a doctor must know not only the illness and its cause but also the nature of the body in normal physical condition. First, without knowing what normal temperature, respiration, and pulse are, a doctor can neither tell a pathological state from a normal one nor determine the gravity of an illness. Second, without data on the normal condition of the body, the doctor is unable to prescribe suitable therapy. The Buddha knew from his own experience the ideal state of perfect spiritual health, free of all suffering. And on the basis of this knowledge he was able to diagnose and prescribe treatment for the sufferings of others. The third of the four truths pertains to the spiritual state that is free of all suffering.

A physician who knows the illness, its cause, and the optimum condition of the body is able to prescribe a complete course of therapy, including such direct action as surgery, injections, and other medication as well as indirect treatment in the form of proper diet, rest, and exercise. In similar fashion, knowing the nature of suffering, its cause, and the condition free of suffering, the Buddha prescribes the Eightfold Path as a rational way to restore total spiritual health. The path, a system of practical discipline, must be connected by causal relations with the restoration of a sound spiritual condition, just as the physician's therapy must have a cause-and-effect relation with the most rational way to restore good physical health. The fourth of the truths is the way to bring about perfect spiritual health.

The Four Noble Truths and the Eightfold Path constitute an eminently rational method for curing spiritual malaise that is similar in approach to the method used by medical science in curing physical illness. In addition, the Buddha's system agrees fundamentally with the scientific approach in studying phenomena—natural, cultural, or social—to arrive at general principles, work in accord with these principles, and apply them to the creation of human ideals. On the basis of an understanding of the principle of cause and effect, the Buddhist system accurately identifies mental actions and fate as the effects of causes and applies this principle to the creation of an ideal spiritual condition. This is the basic meaning of the Four Noble Truths.

SETTING THE WHEEL OF THE LAW IN MOTION

The Buddhist doctrine of cause and effect is purely theoretical. The teachings of the Four Noble Truths and the Eightfold Path, on the other hand, are practical ways to cure spiritual illness. For the Buddha, and for his disciples as well, the theoretical truth of cause and effect was a hardwon personal understanding; for the purpose of guiding others, that principle was formulated as the Four Noble Truths, the topic of the Buddha's first sermon, known as "setting the Wheel of the Law in motion." This sermon, supreme among all the sermons of all the buddhas, was delivered to five ascetics in Deer Park in Benares.

I have already explained how Shakyamuni employed the elementary teachings of the triple doctrine—that one must give to others and abide by the five precepts, and that by doing these things one will be born in a heavenly realm—and the gradual method of instruction to enable his audience to understand the doctrine of cause and effect correctly. Only when this state of understanding was reached was the audience ready to hear the more distinctly Buddhist teaching of the Four Noble Truths. But the five ascetics in Benares already understood cause and effect and karmic determination. Like other men of religion of their day, however, they believed that meditation and asceticism were the sole path

to supreme enlightenment. Indeed, they had served Shakyamuni during the six years of extreme ascetic austerities
that he underwent while he, too, believed that this was
the one way to enlightenment. Later, when experience
had taught him that austerities did not lead to the end he
sought, Shakyamuni gave up fasting and mortification.
Cleansing his body, he ate delicious, nourishing milk gruel
offered him by a young woman. Seeing this, the five ascetics mistakenly assumed that he had abandoned self-
discipline to return to a depraved, worldly life of luxury
and pleasure. Seeing no further point in following him,
they left Shakyamuni to continue their own training and
discipline in Deer Park, where a group of Brahmans had
gathered.

When, not long after, he attained enlightenment while
meditating under a bo tree, Shakyamuni gave thought to
the people who would be most likely to understand the
wonderful teaching based on the law of dependent origination. The two teachers with whom he had studied meditation earlier were now dead, and the five ascetics seemed to
be the only candidates. He therefore set out for Benares.
Seeing him from afar, the ascetics agreed among themselves that there was no need to serve this "backslider Gautama" as they had once done, or even to greet him. If he
wanted to come and sit with them, they would tolerate him.
But in spite of their agreement, Shakyamuni's personal
appeal was so great that each of them was compelled to
rise and greet him when he arrived. Nonetheless, despis-
ing him in their hearts, they addressed him as they would
an ordinary friend. Realizing what they were thinking,
Shakyamuni told them repeatedly that he was changed,
that he was now a perfected, enlightened buddha. When
this had no effect on them, he delivered his famous sermon.

First he told them that neither ascetic austerities, which
weaken the body and consume the spirit, nor hedonism
leads to the ultimate ideal and that both extremes are ig-

noble. The only way to reach ideal truth is to pursue the Middle Way between extremes. He went on to explain that the Middle Way is the Eightfold Path, by means of which he himself had attained enlightenment. Upon hearing this preliminary explanation, the five men saw the error of their former belief that asceticism leads to enlightenment and were prepared to listen to the rest of what Shakyamuni had to say. He next explained the Four Noble Truths:

"Monks, birth is suffering, aging is suffering, illness is suffering, death is suffering, union with the hateful is suffering, separation from the beloved is suffering, failing to obtain the desired is suffering. In short, attachment to all physical and mental aspects of our environment is suffering. This is the Noble Truth pertaining to suffering.

"Monks, the origin of suffering is craving—craving for physical pleasure, existence, and nonexistence, which leads to rebirth into the cycle of transmigration and is accompanied by lust and the constant search for pleasure. This is the Noble Truth pertaining to the origin of suffering.

"Monks, total elimination and abandonment of such craving and liberation from all attachments are the ideal goal. This is the Noble Truth concerning the elimination of suffering.

"Monks, the way to attain this ideal is to follow the Eightfold Path—right views, right thought, right speech, right action, right livelihood, right effort, right mindfulness, and right meditation. This is the Noble Truth pertaining to the Way by means of which suffering is eliminated."

In the course of the sermon, Shakyamuni explained to the monks that he had become a buddha and had realized that he was a great teacher of heavenly and human beings only by seeing that these four principles are totally true on the theoretical plane, adopting a suitable course of practical action based on them, and applying the course thoroughly until theory and practice became one.

After hearing the doctrine of the Four Noble Truths, the five ascetics attained the pure Eye of the Law, which, as I have said, is the initial step on the way to becoming an *arhat*. The Eye of the Law enables theoretical understanding of the Four Noble Truths and the law of dependent origination, enables the person possessing it to see the world and humanity in the correct Buddhist way, and thus results in faith so certain and stable that defection to the teachings of other religions is impossible. It is said that the five ascetics went on to pursue the course of development outlined above and ultimately became *arhats* themselves.

SUFFERING

Buddhism begins with a direct examination of suffering, which figures prominently in most basic Buddhist teachings. For instance, one of the most fundamental of Buddhist doctrines is the four seals of the Law—suffering, impermanence, absence of a permanent self, and nirvana. The first of the Four Noble Truths is that birth is suffering, and in the Twelve-linked Chain of Dependent Origination, the final link, aging and death, is described as lamentable and pitiable suffering. Because of the numerous mentions of suffering in the most ancient scriptures, some people criticize Buddhism as pessimistic or argue that it is too otherworldly and aloof from the affairs of everyday life. But to overcome suffering is the purpose of all religions. The ultimate goal of Buddhism, too, is to conquer suffering, transcend the cycle of transmigrations, and attain the tranquillity called nirvana.

But first human beings must be awakened to the truth that the world is suffering and that a compound of delusions hinders the realization of the ideal state. This can happen naturally. The higher an individual's ideals, the more vivid will be that person's recognition of the inadequacies and sufferings of the world. The great Japanese priest

Shinran (1173–1263), founder of the True Pure Land sect, felt the world's—and his own—inadequacies so keenly that he advanced the theory that Amitabha Buddha made his celebrated forty-eight vows to save humankind fundamentally for the sake of the wicked. This theory parallels the correspondence I have just mentioned between lofty ideals and awareness of the world as full of suffering. The more wretched the human being, the more powerfully must Amitabha extend his protection and salvation. From the standpoint of wicked human beings, the more deeply aware people are of their own folly and evil, the more earnest will be their request for salvation from Amitabha and the fuller their appreciation of the power of salvation when it is granted. In short, the more aware they are of their folly and sin, the stronger will be their longing to attain an ideal state free of folly and sin. From the religious standpoint, it is acceptable to interpret everything in the world as suffering, since this leads people to an awareness of their true condition and to the desire to better it.

Outside of the realm of religious idealism, however, it is less easy to accept everything in the world as suffering. First, in most cases suffering and pleasure are relative and highly subjective. Views of the world differ according to one's condition, including one's social position and economic status. Some people consider the world a place filled with happiness and hope. Other people regard it as unhappy and full of strife. Still other people subscribe to neither opinion. Furthermore, one person can be displeased with a set of circumstances that suits another perfectly. Or, depending on time and place, the very same person may view exactly the same set of circumstances now with pleasure, now with pain. In short, it is unlikely that people can accept unconditionally the notion that everything in the world is suffering, since the possible views of the human situation are as numerous and varied as the viewers. Other Buddhist doctrines, such as the impermanence of all things and the absence of a persisting self, are acceptable as objective truths because we are able to make correct observations in connection with them. The same objectivity cannot be claimed for the doctrine that all things in the world are suffering. Nonetheless, since Buddhist teaching ranks it among the most fundamental ideas, the doctrine must have its own truth, which we shall examine below.

JUDGING IMPERMANENCE CORRECTLY

When he set the Wheel of the Law in motion at Deer Park in Benares, the Buddha explained that birth is suffering, aging is suffering, illness is suffering, death is suffering, union with the hateful is suffering, separation from the beloved is suffering, failing to obtain the desired is suffering, and all elements of our physical and psychological environments are suffering. The first four of these are called the four sufferings, and the entire series the eight sufferings.

From the standpoint of physical science, the phenomena of change, birth, aging, illness, and death are neutral and can be called suffering only when interpreted subjectively. Birth is usually a cause for rejoicing, since it means the continued development and prosperity of living things, including human beings. The death of a person who is close and dear brings grief, but it is not unknown for people to be gladdened by the deaths of those they hate or fear. Aging is inevitable with the passage of time, but it is not always experienced as suffering. Illness is accompanied by pain; but, as nonhuman animals demonstrate, there is no need to dread it as intolerable. Indeed, since pain can inspire people to take better care of themselves and make them stronger than they were before its onset, and since it can lead to great psychological and religious development, illness is sometimes cause for joy. It is the standard by which birth, aging, illness, and death are judged that makes them welcome or unwelcome.

Much of what is called suffering results from frustration. It is only natural to want to avoid incompatible people and to be with those we like. For this reason, union with the hated and separation from the beloved frustrate us and cause suffering. Similarly, frustration at not getting what we want or at being unable to make things go as we think they should go causes unhappiness.

The last of the eight sufferings, attachment to the elements of our psychological and physical environment, is a compendium of the previous seven. Because of attachments—of love or of hate—to things and creatures, human beings develop mistaken desires. But the world is constantly changing, and when a pleasurable situation changes, as it must, the alteration thwarts our wishes and brings pain. Primitive Buddhist scriptures say that suffering arises because of this inevitable, unavoidable impermanence of our world and the things in it.

But the opposite view can also be argued successfully. It is undeniable that the inevitability of change can mean illness, poverty, or disaster. Still, the same inevitability of change can also mean recuperation, prosperity, or fortune. Happiness can come to the unhappy, wisdom to the foolish, and enlightenment to the ordinary person. Once again, it is the criterion by which people judge phenomena that causes them to accept or reject the doctrine that change is suffering.

Impermanence is not itself suffering. Human beings suffer because they fail to realize that all things change. Desiring constancy, they think their hopes are betrayed when they fail to find stability in a world that cannot offer it. For the person whose outlook and desires are mistaken, impermanence causes suffering. In the Buddhist's long-term view, the inconstant condition of all mortals is suffering because all transient pleasures must pass into pain.

In addition to the four sufferings and the eight sufferings, which describe types of suffering, Buddhism analyzes suffering according to its cause in three ways (the three sufferings): suffering caused directly, the physical pain experienced by all living creatures with sensory systems; suffering caused by loss or destruction of things to which human beings have attachments or of which they entertain expectations; and suffering caused by the impermanence of all things. The first kind of suffering is objective. The second is subjective and can be relieved by altering one's mental attitude. Much of the suffering that human beings experience is of this kind, as is most of the suffering that religions are called upon to succor. The last of the three sufferings, caused by the impermanence of all things, is an idea that permeates Buddhism and Indian philosophy in general.

Birth, aging, illness, and death, when viewed objectively, are only natural physiological changes. Our subjective, psychological interpretation converts them into suffering. Psychological reactions often make suffering worse than it need be. We are generally less distressed by illness itself than by the effect we imagine it will have on our future and the future of our loved ones. Unnecessary worrying about such things can only aggravate our suffering. By contrast, a correct understanding of the inevitability of change sets our minds at rest and thus minimizes our psychological suffering. The same is true of aging and death. In other words, subjective interpretation converts natural changes into causes of pain. This will become even more apparent as we examine the causes of suffering, set forth in the second of the Four Noble Truths.

THE CAUSE OF SUFFERING

In his first sermon, delivered to the five ascetics, the Buddha taught that craving is the ceaseless pursuit of pleasure.

He described three types of craving—the craving for physical pleasure, the craving for existence, and the craving for nonexistence—and defined them as desires and actions based on a mistaken search for pleasure and enjoyment in objects that can give no true pleasure or enjoyment.

The first of the three cravings, the craving for physical pleasure, is a hedonistic affirmation of the world as it is and an idealization of the sensuous pleasures it provides. The Buddha rejected this, of course, when he warned the five ascetics against the extremes of both hedonism and asceticism. Physical pleasure is to be rejected because it inevitably leads to regret and suffering.

The second craving, the craving for existence, refers to the desire to be reborn in a heavenly realm. People of the Buddha's time attempted to attain a pleasant rebirth by various methods, including such rituals as bathing in the waters of sacred rivers, imitating the behavior of animals, and other practices. These cannot be regarded as leading to rebirth in a blessed state, but even when people try to attain rebirth in heaven by acts of charity or by observing the precepts, a problem remains: the goal itself is not absolute, since the heavenly realms are transient. They are part of transmigration, and desire for a pleasant rebirth must be distinguished from desire for a truly ideal realm. When the pleasures of heavenly existence have run their karmic course, it is entirely possible to fall to hell in the next life; thus the desire for rebirth in a heavenly realm must be rejected.

The third craving is the yearning for nothingness. It is not uncommon for nihilistic currents to surface in times of confusion. If we interpret nothingness as peaceful eternal rest, it is certainly possible to imagine that people in an age of confusion and disorder might seek this state, and this is probably the meaning of the craving for nonexistence. Some suggest that the craving for nothingness may have arisen from a mistaken view of nirvana, a goal common to most Indian religions. The Buddhist state of nirvana is not the absence of all things but the absence of the mistaken desires and actions that are the causes of suffering. In the state of nirvana, true and ideal activity continues in an even more vigorous fashion. Nirvana is to be found in the world of transmigration, though unbound by its fetters. In any case, though nothingness can be conceived of, it cannot be said to exist. Craving for a nonexistent state is, of course, mistaken and must be rejected.

Since the three cravings are not cravings for the ideal but mistaken cravings, they cannot lead to the ideal. Indeed, they actively obstruct its attainment and only increase the sufferings of those bound in the cycle of transmigration. As the causes of suffering, these three cravings make up the content of the second of the Four Noble Truths.

In the Four Noble Truths, craving alone is given as the cause of suffering, but in the Twelve-linked Chain of Dependent Origination, the causes of the sufferings of transmigration are analyzed as ignorance and action as well as craving, grasping, and becoming. Ignorance and craving are mistaken thoughts and desires, and the fundamental causes of suffering. Action, grasping, and becoming are activities, and the direct causes of suffering. Though the second of the Four Noble Truths mentions only craving as the cause, suffering also arises from mistaken desires and actions; the true causes of suffering include not only craving but also ignorance, action, grasping, and the other causes cited in the Twelve-linked Chain of Dependent Origination.

Buddhism employs the all-inclusive term *klesha* to mean the mistaken thoughts and actions that obstruct our attainment of enlightenment. (*Kleshas* are also thought of as impurities, and eliminating them is described as purifying the mind.) The most fundamental of these obstructions are the three poisons: greed, anger, and foolishness. Greed is desire for and attachment to things regarded as pleasant and enjoyable, and anger is aversion and resistance to things regarded as unpleasant and undesirable. Greed and anger are the same as craving, since craving is a mistaken desire, a mistaken love or hate of things. Foolishness, a lack of knowledge of the truth, is identical with ignorance in the Twelve-linked Chain of Dependent Origination. The three poisons, then, can be reduced to craving and ignorance, the fundamental causes of all suffering.

When the three further obstructions of pride, doubt, and false views are added to the three poisons, we have what are known as the six fundamental obstructions. Pride and self-centeredness prevent human beings from evaluating others correctly and lead to incorrect understanding and actions. Doubt is failure to believe in the existence of truth, the reality of good and evil, and the efficacy of karma. From such doubts are born false views that in turn obstruct faith in the Three Treasures. Of course, earnest, constructive doubt can lend strength to the pursuit of the ideal, but destructive skepticism serves no purpose at all. Such futile doubt is criticized in the six fundamental obstructions.

The last of the six fundamental obstructions is false views, of which there are five kinds. Adding these to the previous five of the six fundamental obstructions gives us what are known in Buddhism as the ten fundamental obstructions. The five false views are (1) belief that the perceivable self, which is only a temporary aggregation of elements determined by cause and effect, is a true, persistent entity, (2) belief in either of the extreme views of eternal existence or the annihilation of existence, (3) rejection of the law of cause and effect, (4) belief in mistaken theories of cause and effect (such as those put forth by other teachers in Shakyamuni's time, described in chapter two), and (5) belief that any of the previous four false views are the truth, that is, taking a mistaken ideal for a true ideal. The obstruction known as false views is ignorance of the truth taught by Buddhism and the adoption of false ideals in its stead. This is foolishness at its most stubborn and dangerous. Greed, anger, foolishness, pride, and doubt are known as the five dull obstructions, while the five false views are called the five sharp obstructions.

All of these obstructions cloud the truth, lead to mistaken thoughts and actions, and prevent the realization of the ideal and thus are causes of suffering. To recognize suffering as suffering and see obstructions as obstructions calls for an understanding of the Buddhist religious ideal. The truths of suffering and its cause are based on the truth of the elimination of suffering. When the possibility of an end to suffering is glimpsed, the true nature of suffering and its causes become clear. Though they should be eliminated, suffering and its causes must be seen as aspects of reality, and the ideal of the elimination of suffering must be realized. Viewed in this way, suffering becomes the noble truth of suffering, and its cause the noble truth of the cause of suffering.

FREEDOM FROM SUFFERING

If the existence of the ordinary mortal is one of suffering, the state of the enlightened sage, whose delusions have been eliminated, is the complete tranquillity of nirvana. In his first sermon, the Buddha described nirvana as "the utter passionless cessation of, the giving up of, the forsaking of, the release from, the absence of longing for this craving." Craving represents all the obstructions, including ignorance, that hinder the realization of the ideal state. Nirvana is the state in which all obstructions have been eliminated and one can function in accord with the ideal.

This is the primitive Buddhist teaching, based on the oldest of Shakyamuni's teachings. Sectarian Buddhism later distinguished two kinds of nirvana: incomplete nirvana (nirvana with residue) and complete nirvana (nirvana without residue). In the enlightenment of incomplete nirvana, karmic conditions require the continued existence of the physical being in the world. Only when all past karma has run its course and the physical body has perished is complete nirvana attained. The concepts of complete and incomplete nirvana grew out of Indian speculation on karma as a mechanistic and substantial process—a proposition about which Buddhism, which rejects metaphysical debate, refuses to speculate. The Buddha himself disavowed all discussion of the possibility of life after death and by doing so ruled out the possibility of nirvana as attainable after death.

Ignorant of this aspect of the Buddha's teaching, early Western students of Buddhism followed sectarian Buddhist thought and accepted the doctrine of two nirvanas. T. W. Rhys Davids (1843–1922), who was familiar with primitive Buddhism, set such students right by referring to the Samyutta-nikaya to demonstrate that nirvana means not the destruction of life but the elimination of all obstructions to enlightenment. The term nirvana means "blowing out." Just as a wind can blow out a lamp, so self-discipline and religious practice can extinguish the flame of the obstructions that cause our suffering. The Samyutta-nikaya contains a passage that explains nirvana more explicitly. An itinerant ascetic asks the Buddha's disciple Shariputra what the nature of nirvana is. Shariputra replies that nirvana is the condition in which all greed, anger, and ignorance have been extinguished. In short, it is a state free of the three poisons. Far from being an inert, inactive condition attained only after physical and mental annihilation, nirvana is the condition in which all human potential is realized in the ideal state of enlightenment.

For the forty-five years during which he lived and taught after his enlightenment, Shakyamuni Buddha was part of the ordinary mortal world. For him nirvana and the ordinary world were one. *Arhats*, who have freed themselves of delusion, have been described as occupying a state in which life has been exhausted and from which there will be no returning to the realm of birth and death. This means not that life and death no longer have objective existence but that they cease to be a problem and that the fear of transmigration in the realm of birth and death disappears. In the first stages of Buddhist practice, some people train because they are afraid of the results of good and bad karma and long for the joy that they imagine nirvana to be. But because they have achieved a state of absolute freedom, *arhats,* who have destroyed all obstructions to enlightenment, cannot be defeated by the temptations of the world. Though they reside in the world, their minds are serene, pure, and immovable, and they are able to work for the salvation of others and the improvement of human society. They give no thought to their own pain or safety, leave birth, death, pleasure, and pain to their predetermined course, and continue their selfless activity. This is the realm of nirvana in which the Buddha and the *arhat* reside.

Mahayana Buddhism insists that true nirvana is a state in which one abides permanently in neither the realm of birth and death nor the quiescence of nirvana and calls this state "nirvana without fixed abode" (*apratishthita-nirvana*). But since this was in fact the nature of nirvana for both Shakyamuni and primitive Buddhism, the invention of this special term was superfluous. Nirvana is not a concept to be pondered and understood intellectually but the actual realization of the ideal state in each thought and deed, accomplished with perfect freedom from all obstructions and impediments, without mental or physical effort, and in the natural, spontaneous activity of perfection. This is the ultimate goal of Buddhism.

THE WAY TO ELIMINATE SUFFERING

In his first sermon, Shakyamuni explained that the extremes of hedonism and asceticism are to be avoided and that the correct way to the realization of the ideal state of wisdom is the Eightfold Path: right views, right thought, right speech, right action, right livelihood, right effort, right mindfulness, and right meditation. The Eightfold Path is taught in the Four Noble Truths as the way to eliminate suffering. But primitive Buddhism provided numerous courses of practice for the attainment of wisdom. In later centuries, several of these courses were amalgamated as the thirty-seven practices conducive to enlightenment, which consisted of the four fields of mindfulness, the four right efforts, the four psychic powers, the five moral faculties, the five moral powers, the seven factors of enlightenment, and the Eightfold Path. This systematization into thirty-seven practices, a development of sectarian Buddhism, is not found in earlier teachings. Many other courses of practice, however, are part of primitive Buddhism and can be considered to have originated with the Buddha himself.

A large number of systems were needed because the Buddha always adapted his teachings and his prescriptions for practice to the personality, state of development, environment, and occupational background of the individual in question. Medicine is prescribed according to the nature of the illness. No one takes stomach medicine for a headache. The best therapy is one that sets out to put the entire physical being, not just the pathologically affected part, in good condition. Similarly, the Buddha's teachings are gauged to the nature of the individual case and usually apply to the entire psychological being. They can, however, be divided into two main categories: a gradual, step-by-step approach and an immediate, direct approach.

The wide variety of human wishes and goals requires a wide variety of teachings. The graduated systems of Buddhist practice for leading people to supreme enlightenment can be likened to the modern educational system, which begins with kindergarten and advances to elementary school, secondary school, university, and graduate school. Educational content is more advanced at each level and includes both general courses that all must take and elective courses to meet the specific interests and needs of the individual.

Graduated practice means that the system of practice is slowly changed as the student progresses, just as a student learns arithmetic in elementary school, algebra and geometry in junior high school, analytical geometry in high school, and more sophisticated mathematics at the university level. Each course of study is a little more advanced than the one before, but all are mathematics. Primitive Buddhist texts mention the following example of the gradual teaching. In the first stage, practitioners master sixteen breath-control techniques to stabilize and pacify the mind. Once mental stability and concentration have been attained, they move on to the second stage and practice the four fields of mindfulness (that the body is impure, that perception leads to suffering, that the mind is impermanent, and that things are without a self-nature). When they have made these fields of mindfulness truly their own, so that they apply them to all things by habit, without wavering, practitioners move on to the third stage, practicing the seven factors of enlightenment. Finally, when all daily activities have, through the practice of these seven factors, reached an accord with the ideal, the practitioners are illuminated, are freed from obstructions, and attain perfect enlightenment.

In teaching the five ascetics immediately after his own enlightenment, Shakyamuni adopted a gradual approach. First he exhorted them to follow the Middle Way between the extremes of asceticism and hedonism and taught that training must be based on a rational understanding of cause and effect. Next he led them to a logical understanding of the correct Buddhist interpretation of the world by explaining the Four Noble Truths. At this stage, his listeners attained the Eye of the Law, enabling them to see all things in their true form. Next the Buddha taught that the five aggregates are impermanent, suffering, and without an abiding self. Directing the ascetics to meditate on the nature of the five aggregates, he made their earlier intellectual understanding an experiential one; with this melding of idea and action their practice was complete, and they all became *arhats*. Similar examples of gradual teachings are not unusual in the texts of primitive Buddhism.

In many cases, a particular level of practice is further subdivided into substages. The Eightfold Path consists of eight consecutive stages of practice, leading from right views to right meditation. Another system, the threefold learning, is taught as a gradual progress from observing the precepts through mastering meditation to obtaining wisdom. The seven purities, an expanded form of the threefold learning, is a gradual progression. The ten perfections taught in Mahayana Buddhism, an expanded form of the Six Perfections, are also arranged in an ascending scale of practices, beginning with giving, moving on to observance of the precepts, and arriving finally at wisdom. We must remember, however, that the stages taught in these gradual systems are merely provisional teachings; the stages do not actually exist separately but are part of an organic, integrated whole.

In contrast to graduated systems, unified systems of practice offer a single course to be followed from the earliest stage to supreme enlightenment. The traditional method of teaching reading and writing in China and Japan is an example of such a system in a non-Buddhist context. Young children of four or five, with no knowledge of Chinese characters, began by reading the Analects of Confucius. As they went over the text again and again, they gradually learned the readings and the meanings of the characters, though the more profound meaning of the text was of course beyond their reach. Their understanding, however, tempered by time and experience, deepened and broadened as they continued to read the Analects through youth, maturity, and old age. Thus a person derived many different things from reading a single text through a lifetime.

Primitive Buddhist texts frequently mention unified methods of practice, referred to as the "one vehicle" (ekayana) teaching, a single way of reaching enlightenment. The Pali texts only give one example of such a single way of practice, the four fields of mindfulness, but the Chinese translation of the Ekottara-agama (Discourses Treating Enumerations) mentions others: the four psychic powers, the six kinds of mindfulness, and the threefold learning. The four fields of mindfulness, mentioned earlier, are explained in the following way in the Ambapali chapter of the Samyutta-nikaya: "Monks, the four fields of mindfulness are a single way for purifying sentient beings, transcending sorrow, eliminating suffering, attaining truth, and realizing nibbana. What are the four fields of mindfulness?

"Monks, here is a monk who sees the body for what it is, with vigorous concentration and right knowledge, and who has defeated the greed and sorrow of the world; sees feeling for what it is; sees the mind for what it is; and sees the phenomena for what they are, with vigorous concentration and right knowledge, and who has defeated the greed and sorrow of the world." The monks are instructed to practice these four fields of mindfulness from their first step on the Buddhist path to their arrival at its highest stage and, following that practice alone, achieve nirvana. Through constant concentration on the facts that our bodies are impure, our perception is the cause of suffering, our mind is impermanent, and all things are without self, the truth not only permeates our consciousness but becomes the activating force of our life. We must continue this practice until we reach that stage. In this manner, the four fields of mindfulness serve as a single practice that leads all the way from the first step on the path to supreme enlightenment.

In addition to the four fields of mindfulness, the Ekott-ara-agama mentions the four psychic powers, the six kinds of mindfulness, and the threefold learning as other unified methods of practice. The practice of the six kinds of mind-fulness is constant concentration on the Three Treasures (Buddha, Law, and Order) and the triple doctrine (giving, precepts, and rebirth in a heavenly realm). The six kinds of mindfulness was a system intended for lay believers start-ing out on the Buddhist path. Of course, the original teaching of the triple doctrine was that the believer should be charitable and observe the precepts in order to earn the karmic reward of rebirth in heaven, but the idea behind the teaching is that through the gradual and continuous prac-tice of giving and the precepts the practitioner will come to understand the true nature of existence, abandon the lesser goal of rebirth in a heavenly realm, and begin to practice giving and the precepts with no thought of karmic reward. When this stage of awareness is reached, the practitioner has perfected the indestructible precepts, one of the four indestructible objects of faith (Buddha, Law, Order, and precepts) and is on the sage path leading even-tually to enlightenment. The practitioner will continue on this path through various stages of spiritual development, stopping short of becoming an *arhat* only because lay peo-ple cannot devote themselves fully to meditation. If a practi-tioner can perfect the final practice of meditation, that reward, too, will be won.

Thus the six kinds of mindfulness gradually merge into the four indestructible objects of faith and from there flow into the path that leads inevitably to nirvana. Since the practitioner is to be mindful of the Three Treasures and the precepts from the first entrance to the path of practice to its final fruition, the six kinds of mindfulness are re-garded as a unified method of practice. The threefold learning and the four psychic powers are similar in principle, and we need not explore them in detail here.

Other systems not actually identified in the texts as unified methods of practice are similar in intent. The meditation on the five aggregates is a good example. It is prescribed as the practice of ordinary people and prescribed again at each of the stages of the path to enlightenment. Even the *arhat* who has attained enlightenment is said to meditate continually on the impermanence, suffering, and lack of self of the five aggregates. Some texts teach that meditation on and practice of the Four Noble Truths serve the same function, leading from the realm of ordinary people to buddhahood. According to other texts, the practice of the five moral powers (sense of belief, sense of endeavor, sense of memory, sense of meditation, and sense of wisdom) leads the practitioner from the realm of ordinary people to the state of *arhat*.

7 The Eightfold Path

The Eightfold Path is a program of training designed to promote attainment of the ideal state, nirvana. Since the Four Noble Truths insist that it is necessary only to eliminate craving—the cause of suffering—in order to attain nirvana, the need for the instructions of the Eightfold Path might be questioned. Our oft-used comparison to a physician's treatment of illness may help explain their purpose.

When we have a problem with our eyes, the most natural thing is to apply eye medicine; when our lungs bother us, we take medication for a lung disease or undergo lung surgery. But in fact, the source of an eye problem may not be in the organ of sight. The problem could result from a vitamin A deficiency or malfunctioning kidneys; and many times health problems have indirect causes, such as fatigue. This is true of tuberculosis, for example.

Each part of the human body is organically related to all other parts, a fact that some fields of Western medicine overlook. For good health, the entire body must be in good condition and the mind calm. Because of this, though Western thought may find it odd, the Oriental medical practices of stimulating certain points of the body with moxa or acupuncture and of prescribing general body massage for eye ailments is more rational than treating isolated symptoms. No matter how much medicine tubercular patients ingest, they cannot hope to recover completely without plenty of nourishing food, suitable exercise, and sound sleep. In addition, they must be psychologically at peace, free of mental suffering, and optimistic about regaining their health.

Since the elements of our mental and spiritual being are even more intricately connected than those of our physical being, eliminating craving alone will not eliminate suffering. For true development, the entire mental and spiritual being must be improved. All delusions and impediments to attaining the ideal state of enlightenment must be eliminated, and the mind must be liberated to work in a free, healthy way. The program of religious practice set forth in the Eightfold Path stimulates just this kind of overall mental development and personal perfection.

RIGHT VIEWS, RIGHT THOUGHT

The first step on the Eightfold Path is right views, or the correct Buddhist interpretation of the world and humankind. People of learning and wisdom in the ways of Buddhism who apply the Eightfold Path as a system of self-improvement may safely be assumed to have already a correct Buddhist view of humankind and the world. People who come to Buddhism through faith instead of learning can be expected to have entrusted themselves to the Buddha, the Law, and the Order and to have faith in the precepts. In other words, they too already view the world and humankind in the Buddhist way.

Primitive Buddhist scriptures mention that the Eightfold Path is intended both for people who have attained no degree of enlightenment and are still burdened with delusions and for people whose spiritual development is more advanced. Furthermore, the Eightfold Path is not limited to

Buddhist matters. It can be applied equally well to everyday human affairs and thus contribute to the perfection of both the individual and society. Consequently, there is no need to confine it to the religious sphere. From the secular standpoint, right views constitute a plan with far-reaching possibilities. From the religious standpoint, right views can be interpreted as right faith, since adopting right views requires people who have no understanding of theory or knowledge of basic Buddhist teachings to accept on faith their teacher's words and believe them wholeheartedly. (The Jainists of Shakyamuni's time equated right views with faith, and so do such Buddhist works as the Treatise on the Completion of Truth.) However interpreted, right views are the essential starting point of the Eightfold Path. Unless the correct Buddhist view of the world and humankind is kept in mind constantly, it is impossible to attain the remaining seven steps of the path.

Right thought, the second step of the path, refers to correct thought, decisions, and attitudes in specific instances, in contrast to right views, the correct fundamental interpretation of the world. Primitive scriptures divide right thought into three attitudes. The first frees the individual from desire and the temptations of physical pleasure, the second from anger and irritation, and the third from harming others (or foolishness, since doing wrong to others is always a result of foolishness). In other words, right thought frees one from the three poisons of greed, anger, and foolishness. As long as thought is right, speech, action, and livelihood will also be right.

RIGHT SPEECH, RIGHT ACTION, RIGHT LIVELIHOOD

Right speech means abstaining from lying, slander, hypocrisy (including causing trouble among friends by saying one thing to one and something different to another), and idle talk (including loquacity, obscenity, and silliness). From the positive viewpoint, right speech means speaking the truth, praising where praise is due, criticizing compassionately when criticism is called for, and always stimulating harmony and love among all people by speaking in a way that is constructive and useful and that benefits both oneself and others.

Right action is refraining from killing, stealing, and immoral sexual activity. In positive terms, it means the compassionate protection of all living beings, giving to the poor, and correct sexual behavior. Both right speech and right action are consequences of right thought.

Right livelihood refers to a proper means of earning a living. The primitive scriptures prohibit monks from practicing certain occupations. The first is work that requires looking down, such as plowing fields or preparing herbal potions and infusions. The second is work that requires looking up, such as astrology or divination. The third is work that requires traveling. The fourth is such work as fortunetelling or casting spells. Lay people were enjoined to avoid occupations that society deemed wrong. In fact, right speech and right action preclude wrong ways of earning a living. Right livelihood may have been established as a separate category in order to include various activities not easily categorized as either speech or action.

Right livelihood is more meaningful if we understand that it is not limited to social and moral conventions but includes the customs and patterns of our individual lives: making good use of the hours between rising and retiring, working well, maintaining good health. Such a way of life requires rational behavior. Care must be taken to get the right amounts of sleep and exercise and to eat wisely. Though our age, sex, constitution, environment, and occupation must all be taken into consideration, an optimum way of life exists for each of us. If we pursue this life steadily over the years, it will exert good influences on our economic and physical well-being, our progress in academic studies and religious practice, and even our ultimate success or failure in life. People who neglect to live in the way best suited to them bring ruin on their own heads. The Buddhist precepts set forth detailed prescriptions for the way monks are expected to live. It should be a major concern of everyone to correct bad habits and live in the regular and careful pattern that is best for him or her.

RIGHT EFFORT, RIGHT MINDFULNESS, RIGHT MEDITATION

Primitive Buddhist scriptures describe four kinds of right effort—the sixth step of the Eightfold Path—designed to cultivate good and suppress evil. These are the effort to prevent evil from arising, the effort to abandon evil when it has arisen, the effort to produce good, and the effort to increase good when it has been produced. Right effort alone promotes realization of one's goals.

In the initial stages of producing good or preventing evil, tremendous deliberate effort is essential. But as the effort becomes habitual it grows easier. In other words, willingness to make the effort to prevent evil from arising and to produce good is the crux. In religious faith, ethics, morality, politics, economics, health, or any other area of life, people who continue making right efforts are certain to advance step by step toward success and attainment of their goals. Without making an effort to improve, however, not even people who know good from evil can prevent their own downfall. Exerting effort to move in the right direction demands courage. Indeed, the Sanskrit word generally translated as effort in this context, *virya*, also means courage.

The seventh step on the path, right mindfulness, means constant awareness of things that are happening now and careful recollection of things that have happened in the past. Primitive Buddhist texts define four aspects of right mindfulness: that the body is impure, that perception is the source of suffering, that the mind is impermanent, and that all things are without self. For a Buddhist, remembering these things provides a powerful, unfailing source of religious energy for the practical application of faith. In everyday life, right mindfulness means being aware of what is happening at all times and avoiding carelessness or thoughtlessness. It is well known that many traffic accidents are the result of a moment's inattention. When carelessness ends in loss of property or life, as in a fire started by accident or a train wreck, the result is no different from that of robbery or murder—innocent people lose their possessions or their lives. On a less alarming scale, failure to practice right mindfulness can lose a business deal, a football game, or a chess match. At this everyday level it is easy to appreciate the importance of right mindfulness.

Right meditation, the eighth and final step on the path, means concentration achieved through the act of meditating. I will not go into the subject in detail here because I treat it later, but I would like to comment on the relation between right meditation and the other seven steps. Right views, right thought, right speech, right action, right livelihood, right effort, and right mindfulness all serve to make right meditation easier. Conversely, right meditation promotes the smooth practice of all the other steps. The first seven steps may seem to be nothing but strenuous effort, but this is not so. As the search for relief from the stresses of modern society that brings many people to Zen suggests, right meditation ensures a certain amount of relaxation and release in practice. Of course, the total mental concentration essential to meditation creates tension, too. But tension is not always undesirable. Intense, earnest study is essential to mastery of the fundamentals of any field, whether music, painting, scholarship, or the Eight-

fold Path. Intense efforts are trying at first, but with per-
severance comes mastery, and with mastery enjoyment.
We learn to discriminate between those parts of our tasks
requiring total attention and those in which we can be
somewhat more relaxed. The resulting spiritual ease is
characteristic of right meditation. Moreover, right meditation increases our spiritual abilities to the point at which intense concentration and effort are no longer required to
enable us to live according to the Eightfold Path because it
has become so much a part of us that it is impossible for us
to violate it.

OTHER VIEWS OF THE PATH

There are two interpretations of the relations among the
eight steps of the Eightfold Path. One view emphasizes
plurality and the number eight; that is, the path is thought
of as eight stages in a series progressing from right views to
right meditation, like a string of eight beads. This interpretation is often found in the Agama sutras. The other
view sees the path as a whole made up of eight parts that
have no separate existence. In other words, instead of consisting of eight separate beads on a string, the path is one
bead with eight facets. Each facet may be practiced separately, and it makes no difference which facet is practiced
first. All eight are organically welded and function coop-
eratively. Similarly, in other courses of Buddhist practice,
such as the threefold learning and the Six Perfections, all
elements are intimately related, so that dealing with one
inevitably means dealing with all the others. However, it is
customary to explain the elements one at a time.

The human mind or spirit consists of the closely related
faculties of intellect, emotion, and will, which are connected more intimately than the parts of the body are. In
fact these faculties are a single capacity. For the sake of
convenience, we create distinctions according to the domi-

nant nature of the function—thought, emotion, or will—in a given instance. The law of causation tells us that every phenomenon in the universe is intimately related to all others. It is scarcely surprising that in the threefold learning, the Six Perfections, and the Eightfold Path each element includes all others and is included in all others.

The threefold learning—observing the precepts, mastering meditation, and attaining wisdom—is the tidiest, most rational categorization of human mental operations in connection with practical religious training. Its three categories can be roughly equated with the modern psychological terms thought (wisdom), emotion (meditation), and will (precepts). Of course this is simply a convenient correspondence, and there are points at which the concepts are not identical.

Many Buddhist systems of practice have been classified in accord with the threefold learning, and the Eightfold Path is no exception. Varying sets of correspondences were developed during the period of sectarian Buddhism, but according to the primitive Buddhism reflected in the Pali scriptures, right views and right thought are assigned to the category of wisdom; right speech, right action, and right livelihood correspond to precepts; and right mindfulness and right meditation correspond to meditation. Right effort is thought to apply to all three categories. Thus the first two steps on the Eightfold Path correspond to wisdom, the second three to precepts, and the last two to concentration—an apparent reversal of the standard order of the threefold learning, which is arranged progressively as precepts, meditation, and wisdom.

This discrepancy is resolved when we look at an expanded version of the Eightfold Path, which includes two additional stages experienced only by the *arhat*, right wisdom and right liberation. In this system, two stages of true wisdom cap the previous eight stages and correspond to the wisdom of the threefold learning. In comparison with this true wisdom, right views and right thought at the start of the Eightfold Path are more deserving of the name faith. The new progression revealed is thus from faith to precepts to meditation to wisdom, restoring the threefold learning to its traditional sequence.

8 The Threefold Learning

PRECEPTS

Shakyamuni's sermons, as presented in primitive Buddhist scriptures, concentrate on practical systems of faith and action designed to help human beings attain the ideal state of enlightenment. There are many different systems of varying degrees of complexity and sophistication, but instead of trying to explain each of them, I shall deal in some detail with the system called the threefold learning—precepts, meditation, and wisdom—and its relation to the Eightfold Path.

As with the Eightfold Path, there are two approaches to the order in which the threefold learning is mastered. The gradual, sequential approach insists that one begins by mastering the precepts, moves next to meditation, and finally reaches the practice of wisdom. The simultaneous approach maintains that the three cannot be separated, that each contains the other two, and that therefore all three must be mastered at the same time. Probably the truth is to be found in a combination of both approaches. But here, for the sake of convenience, I shall discuss the threefold learning in its traditional order.

In the Pali Vinaya the Patimokkha, a code of precepts

governing behavior, enumerates various kinds of precepts that form the basis of religious practice. The most fundamental of them are the 5 precepts for lay Buddhists: not to take life, not to steal, not to indulge in improper sexual activity, not to lie, and not to drink intoxicants. Stated positively, these precepts exhort us to love and protect living creatures (including both human and nonhuman beings), to be generous and munificent, to lead lives of sexual morality, to tell the truth always, and to lead sober lives free of dissipation.

Other sets of precepts include one of 250 for monks, one of 348 for nuns, one of 10 for both male and female novices, and one of 6 for married female novices. In addition to the 5 precepts mentioned above, both male and female lay Buddhists are enjoined to abide by an expanded set of 8 precepts on either four or six specified days each month: not to take life, not to steal, to refrain from all sexual activity, not to lie, not to drink intoxicants, to avoid perfume, dancing, and the theater, not to sit or sleep in an adorned chair, and not to eat after noon.

The Vinaya requires lay Buddhists to abide by rules that differ according to whether one is male or female, married or single. Different merits accrue according to the kinds of precepts one keeps. In addition to precepts, the Vinaya includes injunctions to live in a way that is right and free of evil in both actions and words and to avoid frequenting places that are conducive to error and depravity.

The precepts are both spiritual and physical training, a routine designed to build the foundation for the concentration of Buddhist meditation (*dhyana*; in Chinese, *ch'an*, in Japanese, *zen*). The body and mind must be conditioned in order to achieve the concentration of meditation. The physical regimen aims to assure general health and freedom from the pains and discomfort of illness and to ensure that daily requirements of food, exercise, and rest are met. Overeating, indulging in drink, getting too little sleep, and working too hard leave the body in poor condition, and the concentration of meditation becomes impossible. The precepts have the same basic goal as right livelihood —to create the habit of living a balanced and healthful life.

The mental regimen of the precepts is designed to rid the mind of upset and disturbance. The knowledge that one has violated the precepts causes mental upset in the form of pangs of conscience and fear of criticism, punishment, or shame. One is worried and ill at ease after transgressing the precepts. Other things can produce this feeling, as well —financial, domestic, or social problems. The mental discipline of the precepts aims to eliminate these worries and create the mental base for the concentration of meditation.

PRECEPTS IN MAHAYANA BUDDHISM

Observing the precepts is the second of the Mahayana Buddhist Six Perfections. Mahayana Buddhism also teaches the ten good deeds, precepts corresponding to three aspects of the Eightfold Path: not to kill, not to steal, not to indulge in improper sexual activity (corresponding to right action); not to lie, not to use bad language, not to slander, not to equivocate (corresponding to right speech); and not to covet, not to be angry, and not to hold wrong views (corresponding to right views). Whereas Hinayana Buddhism concentrates on negative commands to suppress and eliminate evil, Mahayana moves in the direction of ideal spirituality by setting forth the precepts called the three pure, all-embracing commandments: to suppress evil, to stimulate the creation of good, and to work for the benefit of all sentient beings.

In the Mahayana Buddhism of China and Japan, the Three Treasures were regarded as a system of precepts. In primitive Buddhism, the Three Treasures were linked with precepts to form the four indestructible objects of faith. While looked on as objects of faith in India, in China and

Japan they were themselves regarded as precepts—demonstrating the historical identification of faith with precepts. The Buddhist educational practice of equating discipline and faith for those in the early stages of development, such as lay believers or novice monks and nuns, partly explains the Sino-Japanese practice. Lacking wisdom, such people must have faith in the words of experienced leaders and must consider it a moral obligation to trust implicitly in the religious significance of the Buddha, the truth of the teachings of the Law, the social and ethical significance of the Order, and the moral and ethical importance of the precepts.

In this instance, as in many others, the unity of the Buddhist teachings can be demonstrated. Faith in the Law means faith in all its aspects, as a doctrine of truth, a doctrine of salvation, and a doctrine of ethical teachings. In other words, faith in the Law is tantamount to faith in the threefold learning: wisdom manifested as doctrinal truth, meditation manifested as the salvation attainable through Buddhist meditation or invocation of a buddha's name, and precepts manifested as ethical teachings.

In some cases, faith and precepts are not equated but are nonetheless closely related, faith being the prerequisite for precepts. As I said earlier, in one classification of the Eightfold Path the first aspect, right views, can be interpreted as right faith. The following steps—right thought, right speech, right action, and right livelihood—constitute precepts to be practiced following the arising of faith. A similar relation is seen in a primitive Buddhist set of five laws for lay people and novice monks and nuns, who are urged to have faith, follow the precepts, listen to the teachings, be munificent, and strive to attain wisdom. Once again, faith precedes precepts.

Though requiring faith before discipline is sound educational psychology, it must be remembered that discipline itself occurs in many forms, ranging from the lowest and most fundamental to the highest and most sophisticated level. For example, according to the sectarian Buddhist Abhidharma Storehouse Treatise, precepts are grouped in three categories suited to the individual's degree of development. The first category, precepts for liberation through the avoidance of evil, is intended for lay believers. The second, precepts for the prevention of evil through meditation, is intended for those who meditate while remaining in the realm of form; and the third, precepts for people in a mental state in which evil is impossible, is designed for sages who have freed themselves of all delusion.

Ordinary lay believers follow the first category of precepts either as a result of instruction by another or as a consequence of their own will power; they look for such rewards as rebirth in a heavenly realm or at least good fortune and happiness in this world as a result of obedience. Thus the precepts of ordinary people dwelling in the realm of desire are incomplete precepts whose aim is happiness in this world or the next. There is really very little to the second category of precepts, those to be observed by meditators, since there is no opportunity to break any of the precepts while meditating. Meanwhile, sages who have freed themselves of all delusion need no coercion to obey the precepts, since disobeying them has become impossible. For sages, obedience is both automatic and habitual. Their faith is complete, and they are firmly established in the correct Buddhist view of the world and humankind.

Every Buddhist is encouraged to master the precepts of the sages, since their state is the essential goal. Indeed, once the precepts have been perfectly assimilated, meditation and wisdom cease to be necessary. In fact, the fundamental doctrine of the Chinese school of Buddhism based on the Vinaya held that observing the precepts was in itself sufficient to attain enlightenment. A passage in the Mahayana Sutra of the Brahma Net (*Brahmajala-sutra*) states that sentient beings who keep the Buddhist precepts attain a state of enlightenment identical to that of all the buddhas. Here precepts mean the precepts of the four indestructible objects of faith and to some degree include the meditation and wisdom that are the other two types of learning. In other words, as is true of many Buddhist teachings about meditation and wisdom, a doctrine found in a Mahayana sutra embodies the spirit of a primitive teaching or one found in embryonic form in a primitive scripture.

FUNDAMENTALS OF MEDITATION

A brief review of a small part of Buddhist cosmology is necessary if we are to properly discuss Buddhist meditation. Buddhism teaches that ordinary people experience three mental or spiritual states, known as the three realms of existence: the realm of desire (*kama-dhatu*), the realm of form (*rupa-dhatu*), and the formless realm (*arupya-dhatu*). In the realm of desire the senses rule. In the realm of form, there is no sensual attachment, but physical form remains. This realm can be achieved through the concentration of *dhyana*, or Buddhist meditation. The formless realm, lacking all physical form, is a condition of utter calm and pure spirit. It, too, can be achieved through *dhyana*, but of a more advanced type than that which provides entrance to the form realm. Actually, originally these realms were not cosmological but psychological phenomena. They were identified to explain the stages of meditation and the progress toward enlightenment that these stages offer the practitioner. The meditation indicated by the Sanskrit term *dhyana* brings bliss to those who master it. It is a lofty state that ordinary mortals living lives dominated by the five senses can attain only after long training and mastery of the mental and physical disciplines of the Mahayana precepts explained above.

The state of concentrated meditation of the threefold

learning and of right meditation in the Eightfold Path is customarily explained in terms of the four stages of *dhyana*. Descriptions of these four stages are largely the same in all extant primitive Buddhist scriptures, whether in Pali, Sanskrit, or Chinese. The Delectable Discourse (*Pasadikasutta*) of the Pali canon defines the stages as follows: In the first stage of *dhyana*, the meditator is free of all desire and all evil but continues to investigate and reflect while experiencing the joy (an emotional sensation) and bliss (a physical sensation) that come of being free of the five obstacles (greed, anger, sleepiness, discontent and regret, and doubt). In the second stage of *dhyana*, the meditator no longer investigates or reflects but enjoys concentration and experiences the joy and bliss of the previous stage of *dhyana*. In the third stage of *dhyana*, the meditator abandons both joy and sorrow but retains remembrance, wisdom, and bliss. In the fourth stage of *dhyana*, the meditator transcends bliss and suffering, just as joy and sorrow were abandoned, and experiences pure recollection.

Because these brief, formulaic descriptions cannot provide a thorough explanation of the *dhyana* stages, we must explore them in greater detail. In the first stage, the individual is free of all sensual desires whose seductive powers disturb the mind and make meditation impossible and is also free of all evil. This means the individual keeps the precepts, both the commandments that liberate by suppressing evil and various other injunctions to be discussed later, and is thus removed from wrongdoing and delusion. The meditator still engages in the mental activities of investigation (thought on a general level) and reflection (thought on a more particular level). Such mental activities, which correspond to right thought in the Eightfold Path, occur at a superficial level of the mind and are the sources of speech and action.

The first stage, however, is not the total concentration of perfect Buddhist meditation. The meditator remains capable of speech and aware of sounds issuing from the external world. Though the meditator is no longer seduced by or attached to the five physical senses, they continue to operate. The meditator is still aware of and can reflect on physical matter that is the object of sense perception, distinguishing form, sound, odor, flavor, and tactile sensations. Consequently, this *dhyana* stage is considered to be within the realm of form. Further evidence that this is less-than-complete meditation is provided by the persistence of such superficial mental operations as investigation and reflection.

The joy of being liberated from the five obstacles means that the person at this stage of meditation is free of the sensual attachments of the realm of desire. Obviously, concentration is not possible if one is torpid and sleepy. Freedom from this obstacle is essential to concentration, as is freedom from discontent, regret, and mental instability. Finally, concentration is impossible in a mind that still doubts the existence of good and evil, the karmic relation between them and retribution, and the truth of cause-and-effect relations.

Though this state is described as one in which liberation from the five obstacles is attained, this is not accurate. Total elimination of the five obstacles can be achieved only at a higher level of Buddhist wisdom. In the first stage of *dhyana*, the obstacles are merely temporarily suppressed. This general state is attainable through regimens and systems apart from those of Buddhism. Nonetheless, the person who has attained the first stage of *dhyana* experiences the spiritual joy and physical bliss of freedom from the five obstacles, if only fleetingly. Free from sorrow, the meditator knows unclouded satisfaction and peace. In sum, the first stage of *dhyana* possesses the five characteristics of investigation, reflection, joy, bliss, and concentration.

The difference between the first and second stages of *dhyana* pivots on investigation and reflection. Primitive

Buddhist scriptures distinguish among three types of meditation according to whether investigation and reflection take place in them: one with both investigation and reflection, a second with no investigation but with reflection, and a third with neither investigation nor reflection. The first *dhyana* stage discussed above corresponds to the first type of meditation identified in primitive sources. The remaining three *dhyana* stages lack both investigation and reflection, and so belong to the third type in the primitive model. What, then, of the second type of meditation, with no investigation but with reflection? Though not included in the four *dhyana* stages, it must exist, since it is distinguished by primitive Buddhist sources. No doubt it represents an intermediate stage between the first and second *dhyana* stages.

After attaining the first stage of *dhyana*, the meditator advances to the second, in which investigation and reflection cease and thought operations leading to speech and action no longer take place. Free of superficial mental activity and the intrusion of the five senses, the mind is finally pure and able to concentrate in total lucidity and tranquillity. This state is characterized by joy, bliss, and concentration

The third stage of *dhyana* is achieved after the meditator has mastered the second. The meditator leaves behind joy and sorrow and dwells in a tranquil attitude of detachment (that is, with no emotional response), but right mindfulness and right wisdom still remain. The meditator's innermost rationality, which transcends both superficial thought and speculation, is illuminated and preserved, and mind and body experience tranquil satisfaction and ease. Enlightened sages call this a state of abiding in tranquillity as a result of detachment and recollection. The two characteristics of this stage are bliss and concentration.

After mastering the third stage the meditator enters the fourth, in which the physical bliss and ease of the third stage are abandoned, and neither physical nor mental joy or sorrow exists. The mind is emotionally neutral, and the mindfulness and wisdom of the third stage have become perfectly pure. In other words, free of all sensual and emotional hindrances, the mind coolly and clearly sees the true nature of all things. Mental peace and concentration are complete, and the mind is as pure and unsullied as a bright mirror or still waters. Both "stilling the mind" (*samatha*) and "insight," or heightened awareness (*vipassana*), are fully mastered, and the ideal meditative state of equanimity has been reached. The fourth *dhyana* is considered the zenith of Buddhist meditative experience. Shakyamuni achieved it first when he attained enlightenment and again at his death. According to the Southern Buddhist tradition, those who achieve the fourth *dhyana* attain great knowledge and supernatural powers.

OTHER *DHYANA*

Mastery of the four *dhyana* of the realm of form requires long preparation and varied practice in mental concentration. The *dhyana* of this preparatory period are known as the *dhyana* of the realm of desire. Without going into the precise psychological process of these *dhyana*, we can note that after practicing them energetically over and over again, the first *dhyana* of the realm of form can be attained for a brief instant. It cannot be maintained, however, and is soon lost. After a moment of the first form-realm *dhyana* is attained several times, its achievement gradually becomes easier and the experience can be maintained for a longer period. Eventually the meditator can enter and leave the first *dhyana* of the form realm freely.

The meditator who graduates from the first form-realm *dhyana* to the second enters it too through appropriate *dhyana* of the realm of desire. (Likewise, first entry into the third and fourth *dhyana* stages of the realm of form is achieved through desire-realm *dhyana*.) The meditator does not pass directly from the first dhyana of the form realm into the second but moves back to the desire realm and practices a preliminary dhyana on that level. In the Abhidharma Storehouse Treatise these preliminary dhyana are called the "not yet arrived" dhyana (the dhyana prior to the attainment of the first dhyana of the form realm) or the "approaching" dhyana. The preparatory dhyana are similar in content to the meditation for which they prepare the way. For example, the preparatory dhyana for the first dhyana of the form world is marked by joy and bliss, that for the third is marked by bliss, and that for the fourth is marked by detachment.

To achieve a tranquillity even more advanced than that of the dhyana of the form realm, it is necessary to enter the corresponding stages in the formless realm. In these stages, meditators are unaware of their own breathing, their physical being, and all external entities. Meditators ultimately arrive at a condition of total impassivity and freedom from all ideas and thoughts. Four degrees of this state have been distinguished. Detailed definitions of the four formless meditations, compiled in an early period, are recorded in the Pali Majjhima nikaya (Medium-length Discourses).

In the dhyana of the form realm, sensory desire is transcended but physical form persists. However, in the first dhyana of the formless realm, the dhyana of the infinity of space, the very idea of space is overcome. All thoughts of form and ideas of entities are transcended, and no thought arises, so that the infinite quality of space is realized. Concentration is achieved by meditation on the infinity of space. In short, entering the formless realm through meditative concentration amounts to achieving a state in which no ideas of material form, no ideas of good and evil, enter the mind.

In the dhyana of the infinity of consciousness, the meditator surpasses the infinity of space and concentrates on the infinity of consciousness. The meditator transcends the concept of limitless space in meditating on the limitlessness of consciousness itself and enters a state of mental impassivity and concentration. The meditator heightens impassivity in the *dhyana* of nothingness by transcending the concept of consciousness and allowing the mind to turn in the direction of nothing at all. In the *dhyana* of neither perception nor nonperception, the meditator transcends even the concept of nothingness. The very idea of nothingness is abandoned, and the mind reaches the subtle state of neither perception nor nonperception. This is not the condition of the dead, in which no mental operation takes place at all, but a condition in which it is impossible to tell whether mental operation is occurring.

The four stages of *dhyana* in the realms of form and formlessness, eight in all, can be attained by ordinary people and lay believers in religions other than Buddhism who gradually improve and refine themselves as they move from the lower to the higher stages. But a ninth stage, the *dhyana* beyond perception and feeling, can be reached only by *arhats* and Buddhist sages who have attained the stage prior to *arhat*. Though superior to it, the ninth stage belongs to the highest formless-realm *dhyana*. In the ninth *dhyana*, only a subtle, subconscious awareness persists.

MEDITATION BEFORE BUDDHISM

Most religions include a meditative element in the form of prayer. But the profound, silent religious meditation meant by the word *dhyana* is especially prominent in Indian religions. The kind of meditation practiced by Buddhists is not a peculiarly Buddhist development but a widespread custom of pre-Buddhist Indian religions that dates to the Vedic period (1500–800 B.C.) or perhaps even earlier, to prehistoric times. A figure of a god excavated at Mohenjo-Daro, a major center of Indus Valley civilization, seems to be engrossed in meditation, though there is disagreement on what the statuette actually represents. Nonetheless, since the Indus Valley civilization (which flourished from about 2300 B.C. to about 1750 B.C.) is thought to have influenced later Indic cultures, meditation may date back to this ancient culture and thus be some four or five thousand years old.

In the hot Indian climate, people who had leisure and were not pressed to make a living probably found sitting in the cool shade of groves and meditating on various problems of human life both pleasant and profitable. It seems certain that virtually all Indian thought and philosophy evolved from the practice of silent meditation. Though the Vedic period reveals nothing that can be definitely identified as meditation practice, it does speak of *tapas*, or heat. The heat of the sun warming eggs and causing them to hatch was regarded as an example of the power of *tapas*, and this provided an analogy for the efforts of the creator god in making the world. His energy was thus regarded as *tapas* as well. Ascetic practices, such as enduring the heat of the sun, were also *tapas*. A remarkable example of the latter was the practice called the five *tapas*, in which an ascetic sat under the blazing sun with roaring fires on all four sides. By extension, other arduous pre-Buddhist ascetic practices also came to be known as *tapas*.

Probably as early as Vedic times and certainly from the time of the Upanishads (religious texts composed between about 700 B.C. and 450 B.C.), *tapas* was also used to describe a warming of the spirit or mind in concentration—in other words, meditation. It is in this sense, not that of physical austerities, that Buddhism uses the word. In contrast, *tapas* in Jainism has the meaning both of physical austerities, such as fasting, and of spiritual discipline and training, including meditation.

Formal descriptions of meditation can be traced to the age of the Upanishads, when it was known by the term yoga. Later, but still prior to Buddhism, *dhyana* was used to describe the same type of meditation. The practice of seated meditation probably arose in connection with the development of the philosophy of the four stages of life, formulated around the end of the period of the Brahmanas (liturgical texts composed roughly between 900 B.C. and 700 B.C.) and the early Upanishads.

Indian thought divided human life into four periods, each with different duties, goals, and responsibilities: the life of the student, the life of the householder, the life of the forest hermit, and the life of the wandering ascetic. Study was the first duty of the young man. During his life as a householder, he was to accept the duties of family life and raise children to be his heirs. When his sons were in a position to accept responsibility themselves, he was to retire to the forest and become a hermit, living on grains and berries and meditating and concentrating on the sacred syllable *om*. It is from these meditative habits that formalized seated silent meditation probably evolved. The mystical texts called the Aranyakas (forest treatises), the last of the Brahmanas to be composed, were probably recited by hermits living in the forests. The Upanishads, which are the final phase of the Aranyakas, can also be considered a product of the meditation practiced by the forest-dwelling hermits.

A reconstruction of meditation practices predating Buddhism suggests that in the period of the Upanishads, two or three centuries before Buddhism, orthodox Brahmans practiced silent meditation as a part of the self-discipline called yoga. When the heterodox wandering ascetics called *shramana* appeared, meditation, together with ascetic austerities, played a part in their spiritual and physical regimens. Frequent mention of yoga in the later Upanishads (compiled just before the advent of Buddhism), which were considerably influenced by nonorthodox thought, indicates the prevalence of meditation in this period. Buddhism adopted the practice of meditation from the general Indian tradition.

SHAKYAMUNI AND MEDITATION

According to primitive Buddhist sutras, Shakyamuni participated with his father and the kingdom's ministers in an agricultural ceremony of the Shakya tribe while still a young prince. To his horror he watched small birds peck out and eat insects turned up by the plow, only to fall victim themselves to larger birds of prey. The prince began reflecting on the deplorable state of affairs in which living creatures must kill and eat one another to survive, and soon the reflection grew into a profound meditation. He attained the first of the *dhyana* stages of the form realm and passed from one to the next, achieving the highest stage, which was marked by a miracle: his body began to glow with a bright light that eliminated the shadows normally cast by trees and other objects. His father and the ministers were astonished. If this is a historical fact, it shows that Shakyamuni was not only naturally inclined to meditation but also so highly skilled in its techniques that he was able to achieve advanced stages of meditation without any instruction while still a boy.

After Shakyamuni abandoned secular life for religious pursuits, he studied under two of the most outstanding mentors in meditation techniques in the northeast Indian kingdom of Magadha. One of them, Alara-Kalama, believed that the meditation of nothingness is the highest possible state. In the meditation of nothingness the meditator is conscious of nothing. The other master, Uddaka-Ramaputta, believed that the state in which neither perception nor nonperception persists constitutes nirvana. Both men had large followings of enthusiastic disciples.

Shakyamuni studied first with Alara-Kalama and, because of his already advanced skills in meditation, soon attained the same state of concentration as his master. Still, his doubts were not removed. He found no solution to the problems of the human condition and was unable to attain absolute tranquillity. Alara-Kalama requested that Shakyamuni help him in his teaching, but Shakyamuni left and began studying with Uddaka-Ramaputta. Before long, he again attained the same state of meditative concentration as his teacher. Uddaka-Ramaputta freely recognized his disciple's achievement, but the attainment did not satisfy Shakyamuni. He refused a request to guide the disciples of Uddaka-Ramaputta—who offered to step down in his favor—and left that group, too. Not even the highest states of meditation, the meditation of nothingness and the state where neither perception nor nonperception persists, were the supreme enlightenment he sought.

At that time, the sixty-two heterodox schools of thought that prevailed in India postulated five ways of attaining nirvana in this world through various stages of meditation. But Shakyamuni had already experienced the highest of them and seen that they did not lead to the ideal realm or offer answers to the problems of human existence. He abandoned meditation for ascetic practices, which he hoped would help him reach his goal. Six years of asceticism in the forests failed to reveal the answers he sought, however, and he abandoned that, too—though he nearly died before doing so. Finally, after sitting in meditation under a bo tree, he reached supreme enlightenment and became the Buddha.

It is said that Shakyamuni was enlightened while in the fourth *dhyana* of the form realm, a stage of meditation marked by equanimity, pure mindfulness, and wisdom, and in which neither joy nor sorrow, bliss nor suffering, is experienced. He remained in this state for a week following his enlightenment. According to primitive sutras, during the forty-five years of his subsequent teaching mission he engaged in seated meditation daily, sometimes remaining in *dhyana* for a week, two weeks, a month, or even two or three months. His disciples meditated daily, too. The Buddha is said to have died while in the fourth *dhyana* of the form realm.

In Shakyamuni's time, a good part of each monk's day was taken up by meditation. Each twenty-four-hour period was divided into six watches of four hours each. The first of the three watches of the night was spent in seated meditation and periods of walking to relieve fatigue. Only during the second watch did the monks lie down to sleep. In the third and final watch, they rose to meditate further in a seated position. The first division of the day was spent looking after personal hygiene and monastic chores, followed by seated meditation. At a suitable hour, the monks went out into the surrounding neighborhood to beg for food. During the second part of the day, after returning from begging, they ate their food, consuming it before noon. For a while after their meal they were free to lie in the shade of trees or sit in meditation and allow their food to digest. In the evening they once again meditated, went to hear the Buddha preach, or sat and discussed the Law among themselves. The habit of Chinese Ch'an and Japanese Zen monks of conducting four sessions of seated meditation (one in the first watch of the night, one in the last watch of the night, one in the morning, and one between three and five in the afternoon) springs from the daily regimen of primitive Buddhism.

Shakyamuni said that the monks should spend their time in two ways: discussion of the Law and holy silence. By the latter he meant meditation, which was so perfectly ordinary an act not only for Buddhists but also for most Indians of the time that no ancient Buddhist texts explain how seated and walking *dhyana* are to be conducted. Everyone knew, so there was no need to explain. The lack of instructions in no way diminishes the great importance Buddhism placed on meditation at this time. In Mahayana scriptures, for example, the Buddha is consistently said to have started teaching only after having emerged from a state of deep meditation. We have already seen that Buddhist meditation came after the yoga regimen of self-discipline widely accepted in India in Shakyamuni's time. Some Western scholars claim that Buddhism has no distinctive original elements but is an amalgam of elements taken from the Hindu Samkhya philosophy, represented by the theory and practice of yoga set forth in the Upanishads. They claim that Alara-Kalama and Uddaka-Ramaputta were Samkhya philosophers. Buddhism undeniably incorporated influences from the Samkhya and yoga of the later Upanishads, and the idea of the four stages of *dhyana* in the form and formless realms is found in teachings predating Buddhism. But this does not mean that Buddhist meditation is no more than a combination of traditional practices borrowed from non-Buddhist religions.

BUDDHIST MEDITATION

Though they resemble one another outwardly, the kinds of meditation generally practiced in ancient India differed from Buddhist meditation in content. If they had not, Shakyamuni would not have rejected the goals of the meditations taught by Alara-Kalama and Uddaka-Ramaputta. He rejected them because they failed to lead to the ideal state he sought.

In the Samkhya philosophy, the heterodox sects, and Buddhism alike, meditation is a means of concentrating the mind and entering a state free of thought. But non-Buddhist forms of meditation are inferior because they lack the distinctive wisdom of the Buddhist interpretation of the world and humankind. Even within Buddhism, varied uses of meditation are recognized.

The Chinese Ch'an teaching classifies five types of meditation according to increasing degrees of wisdom:

non-Buddhist meditation, meditation practiced for physical and mental health, Hinayana meditation, Mahayana meditation, and supreme meditation, or the meditation of the buddhas. The Abhidharma Storehouse Treatise also categorizes meditation and recognizes its varying content, noting three kinds of meditation. The first is meditation still bound by delusion and directed toward some mundane benefit, such as financial reward, honor, or respect. The meditation of non-Buddhists is of this kind. The second is meditation that is temporarily purified of mental obstructions and attachments. The third is meditation by the sage who has eliminated all obstructions. Enlightenment based on the Buddhist view of the world and humankind always belongs to this final category.

Whatever the differences in the degree of wisdom it contains, all meditation aims at concentration. Buddhism recognizes many methods of preparing the meditator to achieve the four *dhyana* stages of the realm of form. The most desirable method is the one that makes concentration easiest for the individual practitioner. The Abhidharma Storehouse Treatise teaches five methods of calming the mind and seeing the truth, and Hinayana Buddhism, based on the Pali scriptures, teaches forty.

The first of the methods taught in the Abhidharma Storehouse Treatise is contemplating the vileness of things. This is considered a good method for those of a lustful, lecherous character. Such people are to meditate on the inevitable decay of the human body. The meditator can calm physical appetites by fully realizing that even the most attractive, most desired sexual partner will someday rot to bones and dust. When this is truly realized, concentration becomes possible.

The second method is having pity for all beings. It is designed to fill irascible, wrathful people with compassion, not only for those close and dear but also for strangers and hateful people. When meditators have achieved this, they are able to remain calm and achieve concentration.

The third method is instruction in the law of dependent origination. The Twelve-linked Chain of Dependent Origination is taught to foolish people to help them understand how human beings and the world operate. Understanding rids them of attachments and delusions, and they are able to achieve concentration.

The fourth method is right discrimination. It teaches that all beings are composed of the five aggregates and that physical bodies are made up of thirty-two components (ranging from hair and skin to flesh, organs, and secretions), which in turn are made up of the four elements—earth, water, fire, and air. The aim of this method is to reveal to people who cling tenaciously to the idea that they possess a permanent self that nothing in the world is permanent, since everything is an aggregate of elements subject to inevitable dissolution. Meditation on this truth enables these people to attain mental calm, free themselves of attachment to the self, and achieve concentration.

The last method is counting inhalations and exhalations of the breath. It gradually rids the mind of extraneous thoughts and brings calm and concentration to those who are by nature unsettled and flighty. In another system, recollection of the Buddha or his virtues is substituted for counting breaths. Recalling the Buddha or his virtues is a practice regarded as suitable for people of all personalities. It purifies the mind and body, removes all mental obstructions, and promotes concentration.

Pali Buddhist texts give forty (sometimes thirty-eight) subjects on which to meditate in preparation for achieving the four *dhyana* stages of the realm of form. These subjects include both actual physical objects and abstract concepts. Though meditators may begin by concentrating on a physical object in front of them, as their powers of concentration grow they dispense with the actual object and meditate on a mental image of the object. Here, too, meditators select the object best suited to their own personality and spiritual needs.

In conclusion, let us look at the criteria by which the meditator's level of meditation is evaluated. Two scales can be applied: the degree of concentration and the profundity of the wisdom of the meditation. On the basis of the first scale, the meditator begins with a totally unsettled mind. Practicing a suitable preliminary meditation, the meditator attains a slightly more tranquil state within the realm of desire, from there gaining entrance to the first *dhyana* of the realm of form. Concentration increases through the remaining three *dhyana* of the realm of form and then the four *dhyana* of the formless realm, and finally reaches a peak in the ninth and last stage. When we evaluate meditation on the basis of the wisdom it contains, however, we see that superior wisdom does not always result from the most profound concentration. Even a meditator who has attained the highest stage of concentration in the formless realm may achieve no more than an ordinary level of meditative wisdom. It is also possible to attain a high state of wisdom while advancing no further in concentration than the desire realm. Obviously, the most advanced meditation is one in which high levels of both concentration and Buddhist wisdom have been realized.

WISDOM

For precepts and meditation to be specifically Buddhist practices, they must partake of Buddhist wisdom. In fact, the precepts are divided into three categories, depending on whether they also encompass meditation and wisdom. When the precepts are simply rules of conduct followed by ordinary people in the realm of desire, they are called the "precepts apart from liberation." The precepts of the practitioner in the *dhyana* of the realm of form are called the "precepts encompassing meditation." The precepts of the sage who has attained complete, superior wisdom are the "precepts encompassing the Path." In other words, the same precepts, or rules of behavior, belong to a different level depending on the spiritual level of the person who observes them. Thus the steps in the Eightfold Path that correspond to the precepts—right speech, right action, and right livelihood—are precepts apart from liberation when practiced by an ordinary person, but precepts encompassing the Path when practiced by a sage.

The same is true for meditation, which is divided into three types depending on whether its practitioner lacks wisdom and is still hindered by obstructions, has attained imperfect wisdom, or manifests the perfect wisdom of the sage. Since perfect wisdom is inherent in the highest levels of both precepts and meditation, there is no need to teach wisdom as a separate practice or type of learning. When practitioners have reached the stage of the enlightened sage, their practice of the precepts, of meditation, and of wisdom have all been perfected. At this stage, the threefold learning is a united whole that includes a fourth element: faith.

From the standpoint of faith, the enlightened person has perfect faith in the four indestructible objects, has obtained the Eye of the Law through meditation and wisdom, and, by perfecting belief in the four indestructible objects of faith, has attained absolute faith in the precepts. The ineluctable, indissoluble relation among faith, precepts, meditation, and wisdom means that the practitioner may begin and pursue practice from whichever of the four is best suited to his or her character and circumstances (whether the practitioner is a lay believer or a monk or nun, and whatever his or her occupation may be). Practitioners who continue the practice of their chosen path without error will arrive at the goal of enlightenment.

All Chinese and Japanese Buddhist sects teach this. The Pure Land sects, for instance, emphasize faith, in particular faith as manifested in invocation of the name of Amitabha Buddha. The person with firmly established faith will inevitably become a sage, incapable of sinking to an evil rebirth and certain to attain perfect enlightenment. Because of this, Pure Land teachings allow for the possibility of becoming a sage in this life, though the more common teaching is that calling on Amitabha leads to rebirth in his Western Paradise, where one is then enlightened. Similarly, the teachings of the T'ien-t'ai school (Tendai in Japan) hold that a person who is solidly established in faith will be purified in all six senses, will be able to abide perfectly by the precepts, and will attain the first of the stages leading eventually to enlightenment.

The Japanese priest Nichiren (1222–82), founder of the sect that bears his name, advocated total, unshakable faith in the Lotus Sutra and believed that chanting the formula "Hail to the Sutra of the Lotus of the Wonderful Law" would establish the precepts indelibly in one's mind and lead to the attainment of enlightenment. In the thought of both T'ien-t'ai and Nichiren (which evolved from the T'ien-t'ai school), faith and the precepts are meldod. The Zen (Chinooc, Ch'an) sects emphasize meditation, but only as a way of illuminating the mind and of clucidating the meaning of life and death—in short, as a means to true wisdom. Seated meditation, or zazen, unrelated to wisdom is no different from the kinds of meditation practiced by believers in non-Buddhist religions. Zen meditation, regardless of the posture in which it is performed, is intended to enlighten the mind to a correct view of the world and of humankind.

What was the relationship between meditation and wisdom in primitive and sectarian Buddhism? First, at the stage of enlightenment, the sage attains an unshakable faith in the true Buddhist understanding of the world and humankind that is equivalent to perfect wisdom. Yet the sage's enlightenment is not restricted to one who has passed through the four *dhyana* of the realm of form and the four of the formless realm. This enlightenment can be attained by a person with little experience in meditation and still dwelling in the realm of desire. In general, the enlightenment attained by lay believers through faith and precepts belongs to the desire realm, for they have not progressed through the meditations that carry practitioners to higher realms. Yet failure to achieve those stages of meditation does not preclude enlightenment. Ideally, of course, meditation and wisdom progress in tandem, both proceeding to the highest stage. Wisdom without sufficient meditation is called "parched wisdom," for it lacks the nourishing waters of meditation and thus is incomplete. Those identified as buddhas and *arhats* (in particular, *arhats* said to have attained liberation) are those who have reached the highest states of both meditation and wisdom. The highest ideal of Buddhism, unobstructed *shunyata*, is attained only at this stage.

BUDDHIST IDEALS

Finally, let us examine some of the differences and similarities between Hinayana and Mahayana approaches to religious practice and training. Under the influence of primitive and sectarian Buddhism, Hinayana Buddhism concentrated on the Eightfold Path and other, expanded systems that map the practitioner's road to enlightenment. Put to use in everyday life, the Eightfold Path can enhance health, keep people on the proper moral and ethical road, increase efficiency at work, establish a correct view of the world and humankind, and cultivate wisdom. But Mahayana Buddhism rejected sole reliance on the Four Noble Truths and the Eightfold Path as insufficient for its goal, which is to work diligently not only for personal enlightenment but also for the improvement of one's fellow human beings and all society. Though Mahayana followers recognized the value of the Hinayana truths and principles of action for self-improvement, they decried the absence of altruistic ideals. In the stead of the solitary *arhat*, they adopted the ideal of the bodhisattva, whose first consideration is the benefit and happiness of other beings. The Eightfold Path, which cannot serve as a complete teaching for bodhisattvas, was replaced with the Six Perfections as the model for religious action.

The Six Perfections are giving, observing the precepts, patience, striving, meditation, and wisdom. Their purpose is to help all living beings reach the "other shore" of enlightenment, and this is what the Sanskrit term *paramita*, or perfection, means. Four of the Six Perfections correspond to steps in the Eightfold Path. Observing the precepts corresponds to right speech, right action, and right livelihood. Striving is the same as right effort. Meditation corresponds to right mindfulness and right meditation, and wisdom includes right views and right thought. Giving and patience, though important items in the Six Perfections, are not mentioned explicitly in the Eightfold Path. The position of giving at the head of the list indicates the altruistic emphasis of the Six Perfections. Giving is the most fundamental of the bodhisattva practices, for bodhisattvas give themselves to save others. It is giving that makes a bodhisattva. While the Eightfold Path is prescribed for self-cultivation, the Six Perfections (especially giving and patience) are directed to others, clearly indicating the shift toward an altruistic, social focus in Mahayana Buddhism that set it apart from the Hinayana tradition.

Of course, as has been pointed out, the steps on the Eightfold Path have altruistic qualities when interpreted as positive instructions instead of negative commands. For example, to refrain from taking life and stealing, parts of right action, can be regarded as instructions to love and protect other creatures and to work for the welfare of the poor. A proper understanding of the Buddhist view of the world as a network of interdependent beings makes it impossible to act selfishly. But viewed superficially, the Eightfold Path does seem to emphasize practice for the improvement of the individual practitioner alone. This aspect incurred criticism from Mahayana believers and stimulated them to formulate such systems of religious action as the Six Perfections.

Still, it would be wrong to assume that Hinayana teachings did not enjoin altruistic behavior. The triple doctrine of primitive Buddhism encouraged Buddhists to give to the poor, abide by the precepts, and reap the reward of rebirth in a heavenly realm. Later this nascent doctrine of giving evolved into a typically Buddhist practice in which the giver, the gift, and the recipient were all to be regarded as insubstantial. When no thought of any of these remained, the act of giving was purified and truly efficacious. Shakyamuni also taught the four means: giving, kind words, benefiting others, and compassion. As in the Six Perfections, giving includes using all the resources of body and mind to save others and freely bestowing both the teachings and material goods on those in need. Kind words means speaking for the benefit of others. The words may be of encouragement and praise or criticism and censure, depending on the situation. At times, silence may be the kindest and most beneficial speech. Benefiting others includes all other sorts of actions for the good of living beings. Compassion means abandoning attachment to the self and its own interests, identifying with the needs and feelings of others, and acting in others' interest. Giving is the basic impulse behind each of the four means: in the perfection of the practice of giving is found the perfection of each of the four means.

Shakyamuni also encouraged the four infinite virtues—love, pity, joy at others' happiness, and nonattachment—another formulation of the doctrine of compassion and giving. Love and pity (the two roots of the Japanese Buddhist term for compassion) are steps that lead to the practice of the four means. These and various other teachings of compassion and altruism found in primitive Buddhism were systematized and given form in the Six Perfections of Mahayana thought. All six of the perfections are intimately related and mutually inclusive, of course. Giving, the first of the six, is actually all-inclusive. And it is through this most fundamental practice that the lay person can gain access to and finally attain the highest stage of the Buddhist path, the ideal of enlightenment. The giving described above, with no thought of giver, gift, or recipient, is the true Mahayana practice of giving. It contains within it the seeds that inevitably lead to the highest of the Six Perfections, wisdom (prajna), and this is why giving is so greatly emphasized in Mahayana Buddhism.

The two pillars of Mahayana practice are wisdom and skillful means (upaya). The five perfections excluding wisdom are all types of skillful means. Giving, the central and all-inclusive practice, is a skillful means, and giving is based on compassion. Thus we can identify skillful means as a form of compassionate activity. Wisdom is enlightenment to the true nature of the world and humankind, the principle of causation. In Buddhism, of course, this enlightenment is not merely an intellectual understanding but an actual physical and mental experience. Giving and compassionate action are the inevitable and necessary social expressions of this enlightened view of the world. Thus wisdom and compassion, that is, both the proper understanding of dependent origination and the practice of shunyata that springs from that understanding, have been the guiding spirit of Buddhism from its earliest beginnings to its most recent developments. Buddhism teaches that we must begin by properly understanding the way things are; from this, we know the way things should be; and then we throw ourselves into the practice to make things thus.

Glossary-Index

When the transliterations of non-English words appearing in the text are different from the orthodox scholarly transliterations, the latter are given here in parentheses with correct diacritical markings. The abbreviations used here are C for Chinese, J for Japanese, P for Pali, and S for Sanskrit.

Abhidharma (S; Abhidhamma, P; "that which is about the Law"), commentaries on Buddhist texts, 21, 27, 28

Abhidharma-hridaya-shastra. See Treatise on the Essence of Abhidharma

Abhidharmakosha-shastra. See Abhidharma Storehouse Treatise

Abhidharma-mahavibhasha-shastra. See Great Commentary

Abhidharma-nyayanusara-shastra. See Treatise Following the True Teachings of the Abhidharma

Abhidharma-pitaka (Abhidharma-pitaka, S; Abhidhamma-pitaka, P), "treatise basket," doctrinal commentaries, 21, 24–26

Abhidharma Storehouse Treatise (Abhidharmakośa-śāstra, S), 34, 143, 149, 157

Agamas (Āgama, P, S), one of the oldest Buddhist scriptural collections, 16, 22, 135

Aggregate of Dharmas. See Dharmaskandha

Ajita-Kesakambali (Ajita-Kesakambali, P), one of the six heterodox teachers, 53, 87

Alara-Kalama (Ālāra-Kālāma, P; Ārāda-Kālāma, S), hermit sage, 88, 153–54, 156

alaya-vijnana. See storehouse consciousness

Ambapali (Ambapālī, P), chapter in the Samyutta-nikaya, 125

Amitabha Buddha (Amitābha, S), 112

Amitabha Sutra (Sukhāvatī-vyūha-sūtra, S), 28

Ananda (Ānanda, P, S), one of Shakyamuni's ten great disciples, 16–17, 99

anatman (anātman, S), devoid of self, 44, 47

167

Anguttara-nikaya (Anguttara-nikāya, P), Discourses Treating Enumerations, 22

apratishthita-nirvana. See nirvana without fixed abode

arhat (S; arahat, P), enlightened person who has attained final sanctification, 15, 28, 120–21, 126, 136, 150, 162, 163

arupya-dhatu. See formless realm

Aryadeva (Āryadeva, S; fl. 3d cent. A.D.), disciple of Nagarjuna, 30, 33

arya satyas. See Four Noble Truths

Asanga (Asaṅga, S; fl. latter half of 4th cent. A.D.), Mahayana philosopher, 33

ashtangika-marga. See Eightfold Path

Ashoka (Aśoka, S; Asoka, P; r. c. 273–c. 232 B.C.), 3d Mauryan emperor, 19–20, 83, 102

Ashvaghosha (Aśvaghoṣa, S; fl. 2d cent. A.D.), priest and poet, 30

atman (S), self, 29, 61

Avatamsaka-sutra. See Flower Garland Sutra

Bindusara (Bindusāra, P, S), Ashoka's father, 19

Bodhidharma (S; fl. c. A.D. 520), founder of Ch'an Buddhism, 102

bodhisattva (S; bodhisatta, P), one who is devoted to the attainment of enlightenment by all sentient beings, 27–28, 163

Book of Manifestation. See Prajnapti

Book of Pairs. See Yamaka

Book of Relations. See Patthana

Brahmajala-sutra. See Sutra of the Brahma Net

buddhagotra. See buddha-nature

Buddhagotra-shastra. See Treatise on the Buddha-nature

buddha-nature (buddhagotra, S), 32, 33

cause and effect, doctrine of, 47, 48, 54–56, 85, 86–87, 108

Chachakka-sutta. See Discourse on the Six Sixes

Ch'an (C; Zen, J), Mahayana school, 102, 155, 156–57, 161

ch'an. See meditation

complete nirvana, 119, 120

Consciousness Only school. See Yogachara

Course of Knowledge, The. See Jnanaprasthana

craving (tṛṣṇā, S), 49, 67–69, 110, 115–17, 118, 119, 129, 130

Delectable Discourse (Pāsādika-sutta, P), 145

dependent origination. See law of dependent origination

Description of Individuals. See Puggalapannatti

devoid of self. See anatman

Dhammasangani (Dhammasaṅgaṇi, P), Enumeration of Dhammas, 24

Dhaniya (P), cattle herder, 93

Dhaniya-sutta (P), 93

Dharmaguptaka (S; Those Who Are Protected by the Law), Hinayana school 22, 23, 24, 26

dharmas (S), experiential moments or mental states, 24

Dharmashreshthin (Dharmaśreṣthin, S; fl. 3d cent. A.D.), Hinayana philosopher, 33–34

Dharmaskandha (S), Aggregate of Dharmas, 25

Dharmatrata (Dharmatrāta, S; fl. 4th cent. A.D.), Hinayana philosopher, 33–34

Dhatukatha (Dhātukathā, P), Discussion of Elements, 25, 26

Dhatukaya (Dhātukāya, S), Group on Mental Elements, 25, 26

dhyana (dhyāna, S), meditation, 88–89, 140–41, 144–59

Diamond Peak Sutra (Vajraśekhara-sūtra, S), 36

Digha-nikaya (Dīgha-nikāya, P), Long Discourses, 21

Dirgha-agama (Dīrgha-āgama, S), Long Discourses, 22

Discourse on the Six Sixes (Chachakka-sutta, P), 61–63

Discourses Treating Enumerations. See Anguttara-nikaya; Ekottara-agama

Discussion of Elements. See Dhatukatha

Distinctions. See Vibhanga

doctrine of cause and effect. See cause and effect, doctrine of

Dogen (Dōgen, J; 1200–1253), founder of Sōtō Zen sect, 40, 103

dual dependent origination, 69–70

Eightfold Path (aṣṭāṅgika-mārga, S), 42, 49, 82, 106, 107–8, 110, 122, 124, 129–37, 141, 142, 160, 162, 163, 164

eight precepts, 140

eight sufferings, 113, 114, 115

ekayana. See one vehicle

Ekottara-agama (Ekottara-āgama, S), Discourses Treating Enumerations, 22, 125, 126

emptiness. See shunyata

empty debate (prapañca, S), 42

Enumeration of Dhammas. See Dhammasangani

Expanded Treatise on the Essence of Abhidharma (Samyuktabhidharma-hrdaya-śāstra, S), 33–34

Eye of the Law, 48, 57–58, 86, 98, 104, 111, 123–24, 160

Fa-hsien (C; 340?–420?), monk and pilgrim, 34–35

First Council, 16, 17, 21

five aggregates (skandhas, S), 43, 44–45, 124, 127

five dull obstructions, 119

five false views, 118–19

five moral faculties, 122

five moral powers, 122, 127

five obstacles, 145, 146

five precepts, 40, 85, 140

five sharp obstructions, 119

Flower Garland Sutra (Avataṃsaka-sūtra, S), 28, 32, 72

formless realm (ārūpya-dhātu, S), 144, 149

four fields of mindfulness, 122, 123, 125–26

four indestructible objects of faith, 40, 41, 99, 100, 101, 103, 104, 126, 141, 144, 160

four infinite virtues, 164

four means, 164, 165

Four Noble Truths (ārya satyas, S), 41, 42, 49, 50, 55, 81, 82, 98, 106, 107–8, 110–11, 117, 127, 129, 162

four psychic powers, 122, 125, 126–27

four right efforts, 122

four seals of the Law, 42, 81, 111

four stages of dhyana, 145–49, 150, 156

four sufferings, 113, 115

Fourth Council, 30

Gautama (S; Gotama, P), surname of the Shakya clan into which Shakyamuni was born, another name for Shakyamuni, 15, 39

gradual teaching, 85, 92, 95, 98, 123, 124

Great Commentary (Abhidharma-mahāvibhāṣā-śāstra, S), 29

Greater Discourse on the Elimination of Craving (Mahātaṇhāsankhaya-sutta, P), 61

Greater Discourse on the Simile of the Elephant's Footprint (Mahā-hatthipadopama-sutta, P), 57

Great Sun Sutra (*Mahāvairocana-sūtra*, S), 36
Grouped Discourses. *See* Samyukta-agama; Samyutta-nikaya
Group on Consciousness. *See* Vijnanakaya
Group on Mental Elements. *See* Dhatukaya

Harivarman (S; fl. 4th cent. A.D.), Hinayana philosopher, 34
Hinayana (Hīnayāna, S; Small Vehicle), one of the two branches of Buddhism, 14, 28, 29, 30, 35, 37, 39, 82, 141, 157, 162, 163, 164
Hsüan-tsang (C; c. 596–664), monk and pilgrim, 34–35
Hua-yen (C; Flower Garland), Mahayana sect, 56, 72, 79

I-ching (C; 635–713), monk and pilgrim, 34–35
impurity. *See klesha*
incomplete nirvana, 119–20
"insight" (*vipassanā*, P; *vipaśyanā*, S), 148

Jnanaprasthana (Jñānaprasthāna, S), The Course of Knowledge, 25

kama-dhatu. See realm of desire
Kanishka (Kaniṣka, S; fl. 2d cent. A.D.), Kushan king, 30
karma (*karman*, S; *kamma*, P), deeds (good or bad), actions of cause and effect, 27, 51, 52, 53, 64, 66, 68, 79, 85, 120
karmic rewards, 72–76, 97, 101, 102, 103, 106
Kathavatthu (Kathāvatthu, P), Subjects of Discussion, 25
Khandhaka (P), part of Pali Vinaya, 23–24
Khuddaka-nikaya (Khuddaka-nikāya, P), Minor Works, 22

klesha (*kleśa*, S), obstruction, impurity, 117

Lankavatara-sutra. See Sutra of the Appearance of the Good Doctrine in [Sri] Lanka
Law (the Buddha's teachings), 16, 39, 40, 82
law of causation, 41, 42, 136
law of dependent origination (*pratītya-samutpāda*, S), 41, 42, 47, 49, 50, 51, 55, 56–57, 72, 78, 80, 81, 89, 98, 104, 111, 158
Long Discourses. *See* Digha-nikaya; Dirgha-agama
Lotus Sutra (*Saddharma-puṇḍarīka-sūtra*, S), 28, 56, 161

Madhyama-agama (Madhyama-āgama, S), Medium-length Discourses, 22
Madhyamika (Mādhyamika, S; Middle Way), Mahayana school, 33, 56
Madhyamika-shastra. See Treatise on the Middle
Mahahatthipadopama-sutta. See Greater Discourse on the Simile of the Elephant's Footprint
Maha-Kashyapa (Mahā-Kāśyapa, S; Maha-Kassapa, P), one of Shakyamuni's ten great disciples, 15–16
Mahaparinibbana-sutta (*Mahāparinibbāna-sutta*, P), Sutra of the Great Decease, 99
Mahaparinirvana-sutra (*Mahāparinirvāṇa-sūtra*, S), Mahayana Sutra of the Great Decease, 32–33
Mahasanghika (Mahāsaṅghika, S; Great Assembly), Hinayana school, 18, 23, 26–27, 32, 35
Mahatanhasankhaya-sutta. See Greater Discourse on the Elimination of Craving
Mahavairochana-sutra. See Great Sun Sutra

Mahavira (Mahāvīra, P, S), founder of Jainism and one of the six heterodox teachers, 53, 54
Mahayana (Mahāyāna, S; Great Vehicle), one of the two branches of Buddhism, Northern Buddhism, 13, 14, 26–37, 39, 57, 82, 121, 141, 162, 163
Mahayana-abhidharma-sutra. See Sutra on Mahayana Abhidharma
Mahayana Sutra of the Great Decease. See Mahaparinirvanasutra
Mahishasaka (Mahīśāsaka, S), Hinayana school, 23
Maitreyanatha (Maitreyanātha, S; c. 270–c. 350), Mahayana philosopher, 33
Majjhima-nikaya (Majjhima-nikāya, P), Medium-length Discourses, 22, 149
Makkhali-Gosala (Makkhali-Gosāla, P), one of the six heterodox teachers, 53, 87
mandala (maṇḍala, S), graphic depiction of the Buddhist cosmos, 35
Maudgalyayana (Maudgalyāyana, S; Moggallāna, P), one of Shakyamuni's ten great disciples, 54
meditation (dhyana, ch'an, zen), 47, 88–89, 134, 140–41, 144–59
Medium-length Discourses. See Madhyama-agama; Majjhima-nikaya
Menander (Milinda, P; fl. c. 160–c. 130 B.C.), Greco-Bactrian king, 26
Middle Way school. See Madhyamika
Milindapanha (Milindapañha, P), The Questions of King Milinda [Menander], 26
Minor Works. See Khuddhaka-nikaya

Mirror of the Law, 99, 100
mudra (mudrā, S), mystical hand position, 35–36
Mula-Sarvastivada (Mūla-Sarvāstivāda, S; Root Sarvastivadins), Hinayana school, 23

Nagarjuna (Nāgārjuna, S; fl. 150–250), Mahayana philosopher, 29, 30, 33, 34
Nagasena (Nāgasena, P, S; 2d cent. B.C.), priest, 26
name and form, 63, 66, 69
Nanda (P, S), Shakyamuni's younger half brother, 95–96
Nichiren (J; 1222–82), founder of Nichiren sect, 161
Nikayas (Nikāya, P), one of the oldest Buddhist scriptural collections, 16
nirvana (nirvāṇa, S; nibbāna, P), emancipation from existence, 32, 84, 89, 97, 104, 111, 117, 119, 120, 121, 125, 154
nirvana without fixed abode (apratiṣṭhita-nirvāṇa, S), 121
nirvana without residue, 27, 119
nirvana with residue, 119
Northern Buddhism. See Mahayana

obstruction. See klesha
one vehicle (ekāyana, P), 125
Order (community of monks), 16, 39, 40, 82, 100

Pakudha-Kacchayana (Pakudha-Kaccāyana, P), one of the six heterodox teachers, 53
paramita. See perfection; Six Perfections
"parched wisdom," 162
Parivara (Parivāra, P), part of Pali Vinaya, 23, 24
Pasadika-sutta. See Delectable Discourse
path of the sage, 58, 99, 126

Patimokkha (Pātimokkha, P; Prāti-
moksa, S), 139–40
Patthana (Paṭṭhāna, P), Book of
Relations, 25
perfection (pāramitā, S), 163. See
also Six Perfections
Perfection of Wisdom sutras (Pra-
jñāpāramitā-sūtra, S), 28, 29–30,
56
pitaka (piṭaka, S, P), defined, 16
prajna. See wisdom
Prajnaparamita-sutra. See Perfection of Wisdom sutras
Prajnapti (Prajñapti, S), Book of
Manifestations, 25
Prakaranapada (Prakaraṇapāda,
S), Treatise, 25
prapancha. See empty debate
pratitya-samutpada. See law of
dependent origination
precepts, 17–18, 100–101, 104,
136, 140, 141–44, 159; "apart
from liberation," 159, 160; "encompassing meditation," 159;
"encompassing the Path," 159–
60. See also eight precepts; five
precepts; Patimokkha; Vinaya
primitive Buddhism, 13–18, 121,
122, 136, 162; defined, 13, 14
Puggalapannatti (Puggalapañ-
ñatti, P), Description of Individuals, 24, 25–26
Purana-Kassapa (Pūraṇa-Kassapa,
P), one of the six heterodox
teachers, 52, 86
Pu-tseng pu-chien-ching. See Sutra
on That Which Neither In-
creases Nor Decreases

Queen of Shrimala Sutra (Śrīmālā-
devī-siṁhanāda-sūtra, S), 32–33
Questions of King Milinda, The.
See Milindapanha

Ratnagotravibhaga-mahayanotta-
ratantra-shastra. See Treatise on
the Jewel-nature

realm of desire (kāma-dhātu, P, S),
144, 148, 159, 162
realm of form (rūpa-dhātu, P, S),
144, 148
right action, 42, 110, 122, 132, 141
right effort, 42, 110, 122, 133, 136
right livelihood, 42, 110, 122, 132–
33, 136
right meditation, 42, 110, 122,
134–35, 136, 144–45
right mindfulness, 42, 110, 122,
133–34, 136, 147
right speech, 42, 110, 122, 131–32,
136, 141
right thought, 42, 110, 122, 131,
136, 142, 145
right views, 42, 110, 122, 130–31,
136, 141, 142
rupa-dhatu. See realm of form

Saddharma-pundarika-sutra. See
Lotus Sutra
sage path. See path of the sage
Samannaphala-sutta. See Sutra on
the Fruits of the Life of a Recluse
samatha. See "stilling the mind"
Samdhinirmochana-sutra. See Sutra of Profound Understanding
Samghabhadra (Saṁghabhadra, S;
fl. 5th cent. A.D.), Hinayana philosopher, 34
Samkhya (Sāṁkhya, S), Hindu
school of philosophy, 156
samvega (saṁvega, P, S), religious
spirit, 93–94
Samyukta-agama (Saṁyukta-āga-
ma, S), Grouped Discourses,
22
Samyuktabhidharma-hridaya-shastra. See Expanded Treatise on
the Essence of Abhidharma
Samyutta-nikaya (Saṁyutta-nikā-
ya, P), Grouped Discourses, 22,
60, 61, 62, 63, 120, 125
Sangitiparyaya (Saṅgītiparyāya, S),
Section for Recitation, 25

Sanjaya-Belatthiputta (Sañjaya-Belatthiputta, P), one of the six heterodox teachers, 53–54

San-lun (C; Three Treatises), Mahayana school, 56

Sarvastivada (Sarvāstivāda, S; Holders of the Doctrine That All Is), Hinayana school, 19–20, 22, 23, 29, 33–34, 35

Sarvastivada Abhidharma (Sarvāstivāda Abhidharma, S), 24, 25, 26

Sati (Sāti, P), monk, 61, 66

Satyasiddhi-shastra. See Treatise on the Completion of Truth

Sautrantika (Sautrāntika, S; Sutra End), Hinayana school, 33, 34

seals of the Law, 41–42, 44–50. See also four seals of the Law; three seals of the Law

Second Council, 18

Section for Recitation. See Sangitiparyaya

self. See atman

seven factors of enlightenment, 122, 123

seven purities, 124

shadayatana. See six sense organs

Shaktism, 36

Shakyamuni (Śākyamuni, S; c. 560–c. 480 B.C.), the historical Buddha, 13, 15–16, 20, 43, 50, 52, 57, 67–68, 88–89, 92–96, 108–10, 120–21, 148, 153–56

Shariputra (Śāriputra, S; Sāriputta, P), one of Shakyamuni's ten great disciples, 54, 120

Shariputra Abhidharma (Śāriputra Abhidharma, S), 24, 25–26

shastra (śāstra, S), treatise, 33

Shinran (J; 1173–1263), founder of True Pure Land sect, 111–12

Shotoku (Shōtoku, J; 574–622), prince-regent and patron of Buddhism, 82–83, 102

shramana (śramana, S; samana, P), wandering ascetic, 152

Shrimaladevi-simhanada-sutra. See Queen of Shrimala Sutra

shunyata (śūnyatā, S), emptiness, void, 27, 29, 44, 47, 162

Siddhartha (Siddhārtha, S; Siddhattha, P), Shakyamuni's personal name before entering the religious life, 15

six entrances. See six sense organs

six fundamental obstructions, 118–19

six heterodox teachers, 52–54, 87

six kinds of mindfulness, 125, 126–27

Six Perfections (pāramitā, S), 27, 31, 124, 135, 163, 164, 165

six sense organs (sadāyatana, S), 63, 66, 67, 69

skandhas. See five aggregates

skillful means (upāya, S), 165

Southern Buddhism, 14, 37. See also Hinayana Buddhism

Sthavira. See Theravada

"stilling the mind" (samatha, P; śamatha, S), 148

storehouse consciousness (ālaya-vijñāna, S), 32, 33, 65–66

Subjects of Discussion. See Kathavatthu

Sukhavati-vyuha-sutra. See Amitabha Sutra

Sundari (Sundarī, P, S), wife of Nanda, 96, 96

sutra (sūtra, S; sutta, P), 14

Sutra of Profound Understanding (Samdhinirmocana-sūtra, S), 33

Sutra of the Appearance of the Good Doctrine in [Sri] Lanka (Lankāvatāra-sūtra, S), 33

Sutra of the Brahma Net (Brahma-jāla-sūtra, S), 143

Sutra of the Great Decease. See Mahaparinibbana-sutta; Mahaparinirvana-sutra

Sutra of the Tathagata Treasury (Tathāgatagarbha-sūtra, S), 32–33

Sutra on Mahayana Abhidharma (*Mahāyāna-abhidharma-sūtra*, S), 33

Sutra on That Which Neither Increases Nor Decreases (*Pu-tseng pu-chien-ching*, C), 32–33

Sutra on the Fruits of the Life of a Recluse (*Sāmaññaphala-sutta*, P), 52–53

Sutra-pitaka (Sūtra-piṭaka, S), "sermon basket," 16

sutta. *See* sutra

Sutta-pitaka (Sutta-piṭaka, P), "sermon basket," 16, 21–22

Sutta-vibhanga (Sutta-vibhaṅga, P), part of Pali Vinaya, 23, 24

Tantric Buddhism, 35–36

tapas (S), "heat," 151

Tathagatagarbha-sutra. See Sutra of the Tathagata Treasury

Tendai. *See* T'ien-t'ai

ten fundamental obstructions, 118

ten good deeds, 141

ten perfections, 124

Theravada (Theravāda, P; Sthavira, S; Teaching of the Elders), Hinayana school, 18, 19–20, 23, 32, 35, 37, 56, 57

Third Council, 19–20

thirty-seven practices conducive to enlightenment, 122

three cravings, 116–17

threefold circle of purity (doctrine), 103

threefold learning, 124, 125, 126–27, 135, 136–37, 139–62

three poisons, 117–18, 120

three pure, all-embracing commandments, 141

three realms of existence, 144. *See also* formless realm; realm of desire; realm of form

three seals of the Law, 42, 44–50, 81

three sufferings, 115

Three Treasures, 39–41, 82, 83, 99, 100, 104, 126, 141–42

T'ien-t'ai (C; Tendai, J), Mahayana school, 52, 161

Treatise. *See* Prakaranapada

Treatise Following the True Teachings of the Abhidharma (*Abhidharma-nyāyānusāra-śāstra*, S), 34

Treatise on the Buddha-nature (*Buddhagotra-śāstra*, S), 33

Treatise on the Completion of Truth (*Satyasiddhi-śāstra*, S), 34, 131

Treatise on the Essence of Abhidharma (*Abhidharma-hṛdaya-śāstra*, S), 33–34

Treatise on the Establishment of the Doctrine of Consciousness Only (*Vijñaptimātratāsiddhi-śāstra*, S), 33

Treatise on the Jewel-nature (*Ratnagotravibhāga-mahāyanōttara-tantra-śāstra*, S), 33

Treatise on the Middle (*Mādhyamika-śāstra*, S), 29

Treatise on the Stages of Yoga Practice (*Yogācārabhūmi-śāstra*, S), 33

Tripitaka (Tripiṭaka, S; Tipiṭaka, P), defined, 21

triple doctrine, 84, 85, 92, 98, 101–4, 108, 126, 164

trishna. See craving

True Pure Land (Jōdo Shin, J), Mahayana sect, 94

Twelve-linked Chain of Dependent Origination, 50, 55, 57, 59, 60, 62–63, 64, 65, 69, 70, 111, 117, 158

Uddaka-Ramaputta (Uddaka-Rāmaputta, P; Udraka-Rāmaputra, S), hermit sage, 88, 153, 154, 156

Upali (Upāli, P, S), one of Shakyamuni's ten great disciples, 16–17

upaya. See skillful means

Vajrashekhara-sutra. See Diamond Peak Sutra
Vajrayana (Vajrayāna, S; Thunderbolt Vehicle), Mahayana school, 35
Vasubandhu (S; fl. latter half of 4th cent. A.D.), Mahayana philosopher, 33, 34
Vibhanga (Vibhanga, P), Distinctions, 24, 25
Vijnanakaya (Vijñānakāya, S), Group on Consciousness, 25
Vijnanavada school. *See* Yogachara
Vijnaptimatratasiddhi-shastra. See Treatise on the Establishment of the Doctrine of Consciousness Only
Vimalakirti Sutra (*Vimalakīrti-nirdeśa-sūtra,* S), 28
Vinaya (P, S), precepts, 14, 139–40
Vinaya-pitaka (Vīnaya-pitaka, P, S), "precepts basket," 16, 17, 23–24
vipassana. See "insight"

virya (S), effort, courage, 133
void. *See shunyata*

wisdom (*prajñā,* S), 32, 124, 136, 159–62, 165
wu (C), not, 47
Wu Ti (C; r. 502–49), Liang emperor, 102

Yamaka (P), Book of Pairs, 25
yoga (S), meditation, 151–52
Yogachara (Yogācāra, S, Yoga Practice; *also* Consciousness Only, Vijñanavāda, S), Mahayana school, 33, 34, 65–66
Yogacharabhumi-shastra. See Treatise on the Stages of Yoga Practice
Yoga Practice school. *See* Yogachara

zazen (J), seated meditation, 161
zen. See meditation
Zen (J; Ch'an, C), Mahayana school, 102, 140–41, 155